Programmer's Guide To Kotlin

Mike James

I/O Press
I Programmer Library

ISBN Paperback: 978-1871962536
First Edition
Revision 1 July, 2018

Published by IO Press   www.iopress.info
in association with I Programmer   www.i-programmer.info

Preface

Kotlin is sometimes described as just a better Java, and it is. This doesn't make it any less deserving of our attention. Kotlin doesn't really introduce any new ideas that will revolutionize the way we program, but it does its best to be an easy to use language that allows programmers to express their ideas in as direct a fashion as possible, and for this it deserves every bit of admiration that an academically advanced language receives.

Until recently Kotlin was a take it or leave it language in the sense that, if you happened to stumble across it then you might well decide that it was a good idea. Going beyond this "good idea" status and using it in projects remained a fine decision between retaining existing Java skills and gaining the new efficiencies of Kotlin. However, now that Google has introduced Kotlin as its default language for new Android projects, suddenly Kotlin doesn't look quite so "take it or leave it". With a backer the size of Google, and an environment as important as Android, it has become a choice you should not turn down

In short, you need to learn Kotlin, and this is what this book is about.

Kotlin is based on Java so it is an advantage in learning it if you already know Java. It is also a disadvantage because those Java ways of doing things often get in the way; like old habits they die hard. In this book you will find out how to think about Kotlin's way of doing things and why it is an attempt to make the creation of better code easier. In fact, it is an attempt to make the creation of any code easier. You still have to apply quality control if you want your code to be the best it can be – you can write poor code in Kotlin if you try. This is the reason you need to understand the intent of the new Kotlin features.

You won't find any big case studies used as examples in this book. The idea that an example should be as simple as possible to show the idea but no simpler is a good principle. Here the objective is always to show how things work as clearly as possible.

This book isn't about programming Android apps in Kotlin. Android is a complex system and learning how to cope with it is enough of a challenge without also making the new language a learning topic. Learn Kotlin, in depth, in this book and you can concentrate on Android later, perhaps with the help of my companion book **Android Programming In Kotlin: Starting with an App** ISBN: 9781871962543, without ever having to wonder what that Kotlin expression means exactly, or if there might be a better way to implement it.

This book is an updated and revised version of *The Programmer's Guide to Kotlin* which appeared first on www.i-programmer.info.

To keep informed about forthcoming titles visit the publisher's website:

www.iopress.info

This is where you will find errata and update information to keep up with changes in the Kotlin language.

You can also provide feedback to help improve future editions.

Table of Contents

Chapter 13
Exceptions, Annotations & Reflection   **173**

Chapter 14
Working With Java   **185**

Chapter 1

Why Kotlin?

This is a book about Kotlin, a new language that isn't revolutionary in the sense that it doesn't introduce any new fundamental ways to program. It is an evolution of existing object-oriented languages, specifically Java, with which it is compatible. It also has elements of functional programming, but most functional purists would not regard it as a functional language. There are many respects in which you can best regard Kotlin as a better Java – however, many think that it is so much better that it reaches a new level in productivity and protection against making silly mistakes.

Put simply, if you program in Java then you have very little to lose by using Kotlin and a great deal to gain. Since it has been adopted as a first class Android language, it has even the backing of Google and this makes it an even better prospect for the future.

But what is Kotlin all about?

Why is it a better Java, or a better object-oriented language, than many others?

The Nature Of Kotlin

Kotlin reduces the unnecessary syntax as far as is possible without introducing ambiguity or making what is intended unclear.

For example, in Java every time you create an instance you have to write something like:

```
MyClass myObject=new MyClass();
```

Notice that you have written MyClass twice and the word new. The Java is perfectly logical if you know where everything originates. The first use of MyClass declares the type of the new myObject variable. The new is a keyword that indicates that some new memory has to be allocated. The final use of MyClass can be thought of as a call to the class constructor – a function that returns the instance of the class.

In Kotlin this is reduced to:

```
val myObject=MyClass()
```

with no new and just one use of MyClass.

It may be reduced, but it is also clear and it is unambiguous. The val at the start of the instruction indicates that myObject is a read-only variable and not to be changed after this. The call to MyClass is to a constructor so it is obvious that myObject is of type MyClass. Type inference is used where the type could be nothing else but what it appears to be. We can drop the new – after all what does it add? Of course, some memory is going to be allocated to the new instance, but we really don't need to think about it or even acknowledge that it happens. Finally, who needs the semicolon? It is clear where the instruction ends – at the end of the line. In Kotlin you only need a semicolon when it isn't obvious where the instruction ends.

The result is that we save some typing and have a clear expression of what is indented. This is how Kotlin approaches the problem and this is just a very simple case; other examples remove even more unnecessary syntax and have even bigger rewards.

The problem is that Kotlin is a language that has features that are best understood by a programmer who knows what the problems and irritations are of using another languages. Sometimes Kotlin seems to be making things more difficult not easier but there is a good reason for this.

For the complete beginner there are many features of Kotlin that are not easy to understand because they relate to more than one sophisticated facility. The result is usually much simpler, but without encountering the more advanced aspects and discovering what the problems, are the Kotlin approach can seem awkward or over complex.

For example, Kotlin really doesn't like variables that haven't got a value – either by design or by accident. Beginners often don't see that this is a problem. After all, why not create a variable before it is needed and set it to a value later on? The alternative is to set variables to arbitrary values when they are created in the expectation that they will get a sensible value later on. In other words you are forced to write:

```
var a=0
```

even though a isn't going to stay zero for long, and zero might not even be a sensible value for a in the program. In this case it seems to make perfect sense to the beginner to write:

```
var a
```

and leave assigning it a value until there is a value for it that makes sense.

Kotlin doesn't allow this sort of behavior!

In Kotlin a variable always has to have a value.

If you really have to do this sort of thing then you can, but only if you declare the variable to be a nullable type and engage in a seemingly complicated set of rules that governs how nullable types are used.

This seems much more complicated than the direct approach, but despite the beginners doubt it is worth the extra complication. The reason is that when you start to be more sophisticated, variables that either start out life uninitialized or end up uninitialized cause huge problems and are a major cause of run-time errors.

Kotlin is a language that has been designed by a programmer who knows how things go wrong, and because of this it is mostly a better language.

However, this does create a problem because Kotlin is designed to deal with more advanced situations from the word go. This means that when introducing the language even a simple and frequently used construct often needs to make reference to more sophisticated ideas in order for you to understand it fully.

The Kotlin Principle

OK, so Kotlin has features that try to protect you from yourself, but what else?

The overwhelming principle behind Kotlin is that if you find yourself typing the same "boiler plate" code over and over again, then there is probably a better way to express what is required. In languages like Java features have been added to the original language that have maintained the way that it works and extended it. Often these new features provide what is wanted, but not necessarily in the best way.

For example, Java was invented before the idea of get and set properties were fully accepted by the object-oriented community. As a result it has fields i.e. members that are variables and directly accessed. Properties have get and set functions which are used to retrieve and set the current value of the property. How did Java add properties? In simple terms it didn't. Instead a convention grew up that you would manually create functions called getProperty and setProperty(value). This works but it is more work than having the language automatically generate getter and setter functions for you. This is exactly what Kotlin does, and it takes the pressure off the hard-pressed programmer by not making more work than is necessary.

Kotlin has had the advantage of seeing how Java evolved and even in seeing how other languages improved on what it had to offer. As a result Kotlin has provided many of the same facilities but without the need for repetitious boiler plate code. However, Kotlin hasn't been completely free to develop in whatever way was best. Kotlin is 100% Java compatible. What this means is that you can use compiled Java code from Kotlin very easily. Sometimes you have to give up some nice Kotlin feature, but it is usually easier to use a Java library from Kotlin than it is from Java!

The way that this all works is that Kotlin invents new syntax and then compiles it to what the equivalent Java boiler plate code would have produced. As in this case Kotlin is targeting the JVM (Java Virtual Machine), it even produces the same byte code that the Java would have, making it possible for Java to access Kotlin libraries and code in general. This is a far less common requirement but it still works.

In other words, the Kotlin principle is to make use of good compile-time syntax to generate the same run-time code that the equivalent Java would have produced.

You could say that this makes the difference between Kotlin and Java just skin deep. This is true, but don't think this is a small difference – it isn't, because it can save you a lot of time and bugs.

Getting Started

The most obvious way to get started with Kotlin is to download and install the latest community edition of IntelliJ IDEA from the JetBrains website. There is no point in going over how to install IntelliJ – it's easy and can change rapidly so check the website.

IntelliJ is also easy to use and, as long as you have used an IDE before, it should be obvious. There are lots of nice features of IntelliJ that will make your use of Kotlin much easier, but you don't have to use them to get started and the best way is to explore IntelliJ as you program.

The big alternative to IntelliJ is Android Studio, which is an IDE targeting Android derived from IntelliJ. Android Studio is essentially IntelliJ with extras such as a layout designer for Android. It lets you create Android projects that are 100% Kotlin or mix Kotlin with Java. For general Kotlin development Android Studio is not as easy to use as IntelliJ.

Use IntelliJ if you want to use Kotlin for general development, and Android Studio if you are targeting Android – they are very similar environments.

This book doesn't cover Android development, which is covered in detail in: *Android Programming In Kotlin: Starting with an App* ISBN: 9781871962543. You can learn the Kotlin language using this book and then find out how to apply it in Android projects.

Kotlin can also target JavaScript and native code. Neither of these two targets are discussed in this book because, while they make use of Kotlin, they are running on different platforms and this brings up a whole range of additional concerns, such as the DOM in the case of JavaScript, and what API can be used in the case of native code. So while Kotlin learned here will generalize to JavaScript and native code, you are going to have to add some knowledge to make anything useful.

Idiomatic Kotlin

Many programmers make a point of writing code in the "spirit" of the language. If you don't then you are not making best use of what the language has to offer.

Kotlin certainly has ways of allowing you to express yourself in ways that are elegant once you understand how they work. However, the most compact expression is not always the best way, even if it does make maximal use of the features of the language.

For example, Kotlin can mostly deduce the type of a variable from the type of the expression being assigned to it. This means you don't have to specify the type of a variable when you declare it.

Does this mean that declaring a variable's type when it isn't necessary is bad style?

The compiler will sometimes tell you that a cast or a type declaration is unnecessary, and even offer to delete them for you. However, this isn't always a good idea. What matters is how clear the intent of your program is. Sometimes it is a good idea to state that a variable is an integer, even if this can be deduced by type inference. It lets the reader of your program know that you intended the variable to be an integer and it isn't just an accident.

Clarity is important because a program that isn't a clear expression of its intent is doomed to be the source of bugs in the future. Even if it starts out correct, it will only be correct until someone tries to change it.

In a book that is explaining how Kotlin works, it is often a good idea to choose the simplest form of expression rather than the most compact. As a result many of the examples in this book could be written in a more compact way making use of all of Kotlin's features.

In particular, the type of a variable will often be explicitly stated, for clarity, even if it is unnecessary. In the same way, an instruction that could be written as a single expression will sometimes be split into its components. This should make things clearer.

Remember that when you use the same thing in a real program there may be better and more idiomatic ways of writing it.

What You Need To Know

In this book it is assumed that the reader is able to program using an object-oriented language like Java, C++ or C#. Of course, as Kotlin is a plug and play Java replacement, Java is the language uppermost in our minds as we learn about Kotlin. Even so, Kotlin isn't a Java clone and as such there are things to say about its general approach to how a program is put together.

To make learning Kotlin easier, its features and facilities are described with the occasional unavoidable forward reference to something more fully described in later chapters. The idea is that either you will take the explanation on trust, or skip forward to find out the details. In most cases, as long as you know the basics, then the explanations should make general sense, if not complete sense.

For example, in the chapter on arrays and strings, it is explained that you can construct an array of objects, but the class construct isn't introduced until a later chapter. As long as you know about classes and objects, this should not be a problem, even though there is much to learn about how Kotlin does object orientation.

Outline Of The Book

Rather than being a complete reference guide - there is one of those on the JetBrain's website – or a complete course, this programmer's guide is exactly that, a guide. It explains what is puzzling and/or new to a programmer getting started with Kotlin.

We start with an overview of the features of Kotlin that are most evident if you take the language out for a test drive. There is no attempt to be complete or to explain in depth any nuances of use. This is an overview of the striking features of Kotlin.

After this we have to get back to looking at the things that make any language a language. Chapter 3 explains Kotlin's interesting approach to control structures – for, while, if and when. Next we cover data basics in Chapter 4 – arrays and strings.

Chapter 5 is where we start our look at Kotlin's way of dealing with classes, objects and type. A basic introduction to Class and the seemingly bewildering set of different types of constructor and initializers is explained. Chapter 6 goes into inheritance, which is expanded on in Chapter 7, Type Hierarchy.

Generics in Kotlin are based on Java generics, but they have some subtle twists including the way variance is handled. All is explained in Chapter 8, before moving on to the biggest reason for having generics, Collections, in Chapter 9.

Chapters 10 and 11 deal with Kotlin's functions. If there is one single thing you can pick out that makes Kotlin different from Java, it is that it goes to great efforts to make functions entities in their own right. In Kotlin you can have functions that are not methods of some class or object. This is just the start as Kotlin has lots of innovations that make functions easier to use and more powerful.

In Chapter 12 we look at data classes, enums, sealed classes and destructuring. Basically this is all about Kotlin features that help with representing and working with data.

Chapter 13 explains exceptions, annotation and reflection, and meta programming.

The final chapter focuses on one of the things that you almost certainly have to do as a Kotlin programmer – work with Java libraries. In this case the well known Swing GUI library is used as an example.

Summary

- Kotlin is 100% run-time Java compatible and has a more concise syntax which makes it a more productive and safer language.

- Many of the things that Kotlin introduces are better ways of doing things so as to protect you from problems that only become apparent much later in your use of a language. As a result some Kotlin features might seem over complicated compared to a direct approach – but they usually turn out to be better.

- To work with Kotlin either use IntelliJ IDEA community edition or Android Studio. Both are free to install and open source.

- Kotlin gives you the ability to write extremely compact code but sometimes adopting this style obscures the meaning of the program. You don't have to take advantage of the shortest syntax all of the time.

Chapter 2

The Basics – A Quick Tour Of Kotlin

There are some very basic aspects of Kotlin that you will encounter as soon as you start programming. This chapter introduces these in the rough order that you are likely to encounter them when you first try to read a Kotlin example program. As such it is slightly less logically organized and not as complete as subsequent chapters in order to answer your questions as soon as possible. The intent is to give you enough Kotlin to understand most of an example program.

Functions

The Kotlin principle is to make use of good compile-time syntax to generate the same run-time code the equivalent Java would have produced.

The first thing that you notice is that Kotlin has functions that just float about. This isn't the way Java works, as any functions you write in Java have to be part of a class. In other words, in Java all functions are methods.

In Kotlin you can define package level functions.

For example, the simplest hello world is:

```
fun main(args: Array<String>){
 println("Hello World")
}
```

You can see that we define a function using `fun` and curly brackets. You can also see that `:type` is how you define the type of a variable. Kotlin is strongly-typed, but the compiler uses type inference and you can leave out type declarations a lot of the time. Most Java programmers moving to Kotlin don't leave out type declarations because it is what they are used to. Sometimes an explicit type declaration makes the code clearer, and sometime is just makes it look more complex.

All is simple so far, but how can Kotlin support package level functions and still be compatible with Java and the JVM?

Easy, they aren't really naked functions. The compiler translates them to static methods of a Java class called *packagename.filename*, where *filename* is the name of the file including the Kt. So, if the hello world was stored in a file called Hello.kt, the class is demo.HelloKt assuming the package is called demo

This means that to call main from a Java program you would use:

```
demo.main();
```

You can change the name of the default class using an annotation:

```
@file:JvmName("class name")
```

This use of a default class is how Kotlin implements all other instances of functions that don't seem to belong to a class.

Once you have seen how to declare a function, you can almost guess the rest. You can specify a return type or the special type Unit if it doesn't return a value.

Functions are something that Kotlin excels in and Chapters 10 and 11 are dedicated to explaining all of their features. However, a quick look at any Kotlin code soon reveals the following.

You can use a single expression to define a function:

```
fun sum(a: Int, b: Int): Int =a+b
```

and, as long as the return type is obvious, you don't need to declare it. You always need to declare it if the function has a body, unless it is Unit.

You can use default and named arguments:

```
fun sum(a: Int, b: Int=1): Int{
  return a+b
}
```

You can then call the function using:

```
sum(1)
```

to get the result 2 or use:

```
sum(a=1,b=2)
```

to get the result 3.

You can't use named parameters to call Java functions.

Semicolons?

You might be wondering where the semicolon line ending has gone that is so much a feature of the majority of modern languages?

The simple answer is that Kotlin doesn't need line ending indicators. In Kotlin the end of a line is the end of a line and you don't need a special additional symbol to mark it. However, if you include more than one statement on a line you do need to indicate where each one ends by placing a semicolon between them. For example:

```
c=a+b; println(c); println("Hello World")
```

If you leave out those semicolons the compiler will prompt you to add them at the correct locations.

Kotlin is a little more sophisticated than you might think, because it isn't just looking at line endings, it is inferring where commands finish – it is inferring semicolon positions from the grammar of the language. This means that, as well as not needing semicolons to make your meaning clear, you can split commands across lines without the need for a line continuation character.

For example, you can write the previous one-line example as:

```
c=a
+b
println(
        c
)
println(
        "Hello World")
```

If you try to put a line break within the "Hello World" in IntelliJ then it will even split the string and add a + between the two parts:

```
println(
        "Hello " +
                "World")
```

About the only thing you can't do is split a keyword across lines – this breaks the grammar and stops the compiler inferring the semicolon positions.

If you are a Java, or other semicolon-heavy language, programmer then it can be difficult to stop using semicolons in Kotlin. The compiler will often point out when you have unnecessary semicolons and you can choose to remove them. The general rule is to stop adding semicolons and let the compiler tell you when what you have written is ambiguous and needs a semicolon.

Lambdas

Kotlin code generally makes a lot of use of lambdas and it is good to get to know the basics as early as possible. Lambdas are a key feature of Kotlin.

A lambda is essentially a function which you can store as a reference in a variable, or pass as a parameter to another function.

You can use lambda functions in Kotlin in the same way you can in Java 8, even though the code Kotlin generates is compatible with Java 6.

There are various ways to define a Kotlin lambda.

The simplest is to write the parameters, complete with types, on the left of -> and the result on the right. The type of the result will be inferred:

```
val sum = { a: Int, b: Int -> a + b }
println(sum(1,2))
```

Notice that although sum behaves like a function, e.g. you can call it as in sum(1,2), it is just a variable that references the function and you can, for example, pass it as a parameter to another function.

You can also define the type of the lambda, as in:

```
val sum:(Int,Int)->Int = { a: Int, b: Int -> a + b }
println(sum(1,2))
```

This is the same as the first way, but now we have defined sum as a function type (Int,Int)->Int, i.e. a function that takes two Ints and returns an Int.

In this case we don't need the type declarations in the body of the lambda:

```
val sum:(Int,Int)->Int = { a, b ->  a + b }
```

The body of a lambda can have more than one expression and only the last is treated as the return value.

For example:

```
val sum:(Int,Int)->Int = { a, b ->
 println(a)
 println(b)
 a+b
}
println(sum(1,2))
```

prints 1, 2, 3.

As well as lambda functions you can also use anonymous functions, which look a lot like lambdas and hence can be confusing. An anonymous function is exactly what it sounds like – a standard function defined using fun, but one that doesn't have a name.

For example:

```
fun(a: Int, b: Int): Int = a+b
```

or:

```
fun(a: Int, b: Int): Int{
 return a+b
}
```

As explained in Chapter 11, you can use an anonymous function more or less exactly as you would a lambda.

The whole point of lambdas and anonymous functions is that they can be passed as parameters to higher order functions. To do this you have to specify the parameter that is used to pass the function as a function type.

For example:

```
val sum = { a: Int, b: Int -> a + b }

fun doArithmetic(operation: (Int,Int)->Int){
 println(operation(1,2))
]

doArithmetic(sum)
```

The doArithmetic function accepts a single parameter of function type which specifies a function that accepts two Int parameters and returns a single Int.

Notice you can only pass a lambda or an anonymous function that matches. You can pass a standard function, but you have to use the :: reference operator, see Chapter 11.

There are lots more things to discover about functions including closure, inlining and destructuring and these are explained in Chapters 10 and 11.

Infix Function Calls

Another nice feature of Kotlin that you will find in many examples is the ability to call functions using infix or operator notation.

If you precede a function with infix then you can call it as if it was an operator:

```
object1 function object2
```

is translated to:

```
object1.function(object2)
```

For example, if you have a function defined as a method of Myclass:

```
class MyClassA {
     infix fun myFunc1(a: Int) {
          println(a)
     }
}
```

```
var myObject = MyClassA()
```

then you can call the method using the traditional:

```
myObject.myFunc1(3)
```

or using infix notation:

```
myObject myFunc1 3
```

Of course, this example isn't particularly sensible as an infix operation usually involves the objects on the left and the right.

All of the standard operators in Kotlin are implemented as infix functions. For example, you can write:

```
2+3
```

or:

```
2.plus(3)
```

If you are worried about efficiency considerations, it is worth knowing that the compiler translates these function calls to standard JVM operators. You can also override the functions that define the existing operators. The ability to create new infix operators presents an opportunity for writing things in very different ways in Kotlin.

Var & Val

Although it seemed sensible to dive into functions right at the start, because otherwise you can't even make sense of "hello world", there are some more basic things to look at. It is important to notice that there are two ways to declare a variable – var and val.

If you write:

```
var myVariable:Int=1
```

then you will get a true variable that you can read and write.

If you write:

```
val myVariable:Int=1
```

then you get a read-only variable which you cannot use on the left of an assignment.

In most cases you should use `var` for simple types and `val` for objects.

A more general principle, however, is to always use `val` unless you are forced to use `var` by the nature of the algorithm.

Notice that although you will hear `var` described as mutable and `val` as immutable, this isn't accurate. All `val` promises is that the variable itself is read-only, and this is a very weak form of immutable.

For example, if you declare an instance as:

```
var myObject=MyClass1()
```

then `myObject` stores a reference to an instance of `MyClass1`. As it is declared using `var` this reference can change.

That is you can do:

```
myObject=MyClass2()
```

and now `myObject` references an instance of `MyClass2`.

If you had defined `myObject` as:

```
val myObject=MyClass1()
```

then `myObject` would be read-only and:

```
myObject=MyClass2()
```

would be indicated as a compile time error because you are trying to change the contents of `myObject`, which is read-only.

As most of the time you don't change object references, it is a good idea to use `val` on all variables that are used in object declarations.

Notice, however, that the object instance that `myObject` references can have its properties changed even if referenced by a `val`.

So:

```
val myObject=MyClass1()
myObject.myproperty=10
```

works even though `myObject` is read-only.

That is, `val` makes the contents of `myObject` immutable but doesn't make what `myObject` references immutable.

Simple Types & Operators

In terms of simple types Kotlin has everything you would expect:

Type	Bit width
Double	64
Float	32
Long	64
Int	32
Short	16
Byte	8

These types are compatible with the types of the same name in Java.

You can use decimal, hex and binary constants but octal is banned because o or O looks like a zero and can lead to errors. Some examples are:

```
0xFF - hex 255
0b10 - binary 2
```

You also need to know that a Long integer is signified by a trailing L and floats are signified by a trailing F.

A nice touch, though not essential, is that you can break up numeric literals with underscores for readability:

```
0xFF_FF_FF_FF
```

You can also use Char for characters encoded using Unicode, just like Java, but you cannot use Char in arithmetic expressions. That is, unlike Java, Char is not a numeric type.

You can also use Booleans with true and false values. The standard Boolean operations are the same as Java:

|| lazy OR

&& lazy AND

! Not

Although this is a little advanced, it is worth mentioning now that while Kotlin has bitwise operations it doesn't associate them with operator symbols as Java does.

The complete list of bitwise operations, available only for `Int` and `Long`, is:

`shl()`	signed shift left	<<
`shr()`	signed shift right	>>
`ushr()`	unsigned shift right	>>>
`and()`	bitwise and	&
`or()`	bitwise or	|
`xor()`	bitwise xor	^
`inv()`	bitwise inversion	~

The symbols listed to the right are the Java operators that do the same job – you can't use them in Kotlin. Of course, you can use all of the these functions as infix operators:

```
a or b
1 shr 2
```

Null Safety

One of the most important features of Kotlin is that it eliminates the null reference error and you can't meet null safety early enough.

References can be either non-nullable or nullable.

If you declare a variable in the usual way you get a non-nullable:

```
var myVariable:sometype= something
```

and you cannot set the variable to null as:

```
myVariable=null
```

throws a compiler error.

The compiler tracks operations that could generate a null, and flags any operation that could possibly set a non-nullable variable to null. For example, if a function could return a null, you cannot assign it to a non-nullable. This often occurs if you are trying to use a Java function which, of course, doesn't support non-nullable types.

If you need a nullable reference then you have to explicitly declare it using ?
as in:

```
var myVariable:sometype?=something
```

Now myVariable can be set to null, i.e.:

```
myVariable=null
```

works without a compiler error or warning.

To avoid accidentally using a null reference the compiler will throw an error
if you try to use a nullable without first checking that it is non-null.

For example:

```
var a:Int=1
var b=a+1
```

works without any problems as a can never be null as it is a non-nullable,
but:

```
var a:Int?=1
var b=a+1
```

generates a compiler error because you are adding one to a without checking
that it isn't null.

To use a nullable variable you can test for null using an if statement:

```
 var a: Int? = 1
 var b:Int=1
 if(a!=null){
     b=a+1
 }
```

This compiles and you can be sure that a isn't null when the addition is
performed.

Alternatively, if you are accessing a property then you can use the safe call
operator ?.

For example:

```
var b=a?.plus(1)
```

Here, if a isn't null then b is set to 2, but if a is null then b is set to null.

There are a few small things to notice about this example – by type inference
b is a nullable type:

```
var b:Int?=a?.plus(1)
```

and nullable simple types are "boxed". That is, the integer a is a full object
with methods and properties. In this case we use the plus infix function
rather than an operator so that we can use the safe call operator.

If you only want to perform an operation if something is non-null you can use the `let` method:

```
a?.let { println(a)}
```

the block of code in the curly brackets is only executed if `a` is non-null. Note: the block of code is a lambda function.

There is also the cutely named Elvis operator `?:` which will replace a null value with something that is non-null. For example:

```
println(a?:0)
```

will display the value of `a` if it is non-null and zero otherwise.

Finally, if you want to throw a null reference exception you can force one using `!!`. For example:

```
println(a!!)
```

will either print the value of `a`, or throw an exception if `a` is null. My guess is that you would only use this to test things.

These null handling features make null a useful, rather than a dangerous, value.

For example, if you cast something to a different type you will generate a `classcastException` if it isn't possible. It is much safer to use the safe cast `as?` which will return null if the cast isn't possible.

So:

```
variable as? type
```

will evaluate to null if the cast to type isn't possible.

The advantage of generating a null is that you now have lots of ways of working with it that are guaranteed not to end in an exception.

Notice that a great deal of what makes the Kotlin null-safe is provided by the compiler, which does its best not to let you write code that works with null values that could result in an exception.

If the compiler flags a null problem then don't just make the simplest fix. Try to work out what the role of the null is and whether you need it at all. Using non-nullable values is still the safest option.

Summary

- In Kotlin, functions are entities in their own right and not relegated to just being methods within classes. However, to retain Java compatibility at compile time they are represented as methods in generated classes.

- The semicolon is rarely needed to mark the end of an instruction. Semicolon inference means that you only have to use one when the compiler detects an ambiguity in what you have entered.

- Multiple instructions can be placed on a single line separated by semicolons and you can spread an instruction across multiple lines as long as you don't split a keyword.

- Lambdas and anonymous functions make it easy to pass functions as parameters to other functions.

- Infix function calls can make some common expressions look different from their Java equivalents.

- Variables can be declared using var when they are read/write or using val when they are read-only.

- A val is read-only with respect to its contents but any object it references may still be mutable.

- Kotlin supports the same simple or primitive types that Java does, but many of its operators use an infix function notation.

- Null safety is an important and useful feature of Kotlin. Types can be nullable or non-nullable.

- You cannot store any value which could be potentially null in a non-nullable type and the compiler flags an error if you try.

- Nullable types can be set to null but the compiler will not let you use them unless you have checked that they are non-null.

- There are a range of null protected operators that make working with nullable types safer:

    safe call operator *object*?.*method* returns null if the object reference is *null*

    Elvis operator *variable*?:*value* replaces a null variable with a specified non-null value

    safe cast operator *object* as? *type* returns null if the object cannot be cast to *type*

    null reference operator !! throws a null pointer exception

Chapter 3

Kotlin Control

All programming languages have to give you ways of modifying the flow of control - making loops, conditional execution and so on. Kotlin uses a fairly traditional approach, but there are some exceptionally nice touches that if used correctly can make your programs much easier to understand.

The If

The Kotlin if statement is very similar to the if statement in any modern language but with one small, beneficial, twist that we will discover later.

You can write an if statement in the usual way:

```
if ( condition ) statement
```

or you can use a compound statement to execute multiple statements:

```
if (condition) {
 statements
}
```

As always in Kotlin, a compound statement is treated as a single statement. All Kotlin control statements work with single statements, and hence they also work with compound statements.

For example you can write:

```
if(a>b) println(b)
```

or:

```
if(a>b) {
  println(a)
  println(b)
}
```

You can also use else to specify what happens when the condition is false:

```
if( condition ){
 statements
}else{
 statements
}
```

For example:
```
if(a>b){
 println(a)
}else{
 println(b)
}
```
You can, of course, use the `if` statement to build more complicated conditionals by nesting multiple `if...else` statements.

For example:
```
if (a > b) {
        println(a)
    } else if (b > c) {
        println(b)
    } else {
        println(c)
    }
```

To be clear, there isn't a special elseif as there is in some other languages because you simply don't need it. Writing an `if` within an `else` clause gives you the same effect. The `if` will only be executed if the `else` clause is executed.

This sort of nested `if` statement is fine, but if you nest `if` and `else` clauses too deeply it becomes confusing.

How deep is too deep?

When the structure becomes confusing to another programmer.

A nested if selects what is to be done on the basis of a tree of conditions. That is, a nested if is exactly equivalent to a decision tree. The first condition is the root of the tree and each condition divides the tree into a true and a false branch; the true corresponds to the `if` and the false to the `else`. The executable clauses are the terminal nodes of the tree and which one is executed depends on the path taken through the tree to a node.

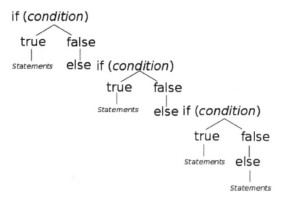

32

A tree is a very compact representation of a decision process, but this compactness makes it very difficult to understand its total meaning. You can follow one branch easily enough, but what about the others?

You can always convert a tree into a set of sequential ifs by taking each branch and writing it as a condition with a single if. The result is a list of if statements with a clear condition that determines when it should be executed. This is a less compact way to write a complex decision but it is nearly always much clearer. Kotlin, like many other languages, has a construct that lets you write a sequential decision process very easily.

The when

One common way to simplify nested `if` statements is to use what in other language is called a select. In Kotlin a multi-way conditional is called a when expression. A when matches its argument against each of the branches and executes the one that matches. If none match then an `else` clause can provide a default.

For example:
```
when(a){
        "s"->println("stop received")
        "r"->println("run received")
    }
```

In this case a is a `String` and its contents are matched against the examples. Note: a doesn't have to be declared as a string, but it has to be initialized. You can use any type for which equality makes sense – `String`, `Double`, `Int` and so on. Of course, you aren't restricted to a single instruction following the `->` as you can use a compound statement in curly brackets.

Notice that there is no "fall through" typical of other languages. That is, if a clause is executed then control passes to the instruction following the end of the when. There is no need for a break or any other exit instruction within each clause. The clauses are tested sequentially from the top and the first one to match is executed and this ends the when.

If none of the clauses match then nothing happens and execution passes to the next instruction beyond the when. If you want a default clause then you can use an `else`:
```
 when(a){
        1->println("stop received")
        2->println("run received")
    else -> println("unrecognized")
    }
```

This is the most basic when statement and if this was all it was capable of it would be useful but restricted to selecting actions based on a set of fixed discrete values. Fortunately, the when statement has some more advanced aspects.

You can, for example, combine selection values using a comma:

```
when(a){
        1,3->println("stop received")
        2,4->println("run received")
    else -> println("unrecognized")
    }
```

If any of the values matches the argument then the clause is executed and the when exited. Notice that these values are tested right to left and this provides a way of writing an or.

You can also use an arbitrary expression to match against. So, for example:

```
when(a){
        2*2->println("stop received")
        c*b+5->println("run received")
    else -> println("unrecognized")
    }
```

You can use constants and variables and the expression is evaluated at the time the when is executed.

As a slight extension, the expression can also be a range:

For example:

```
var a=8
when(a){
        in 1..10 ->println("1 to 10")
        !in 1..5 ->println("not 1 to 10")
        }
```

in 1..10 is true as the variable a is in 1 to 10 and !in 1..5 is true if a is not in 1 to 5. You might think, at first, that the second message in the println is a typo and should be "not in 1 to 5", but it illustrates the scope for getting things wrong when writing even simple conditions. The first clause is executed if a is in the range 1 to 10 and then the when is exited. This means that the second clause is only tested if a isn't in the range 1 to 10. Thus the second clause only executes if a isn't in the range 1 to 10 since any value not in 1 to 10 is not in 1 to 5. Tricky isn't it!

For more on ranges see the for loop later in this chapter.

The most general form of a when is using full conditional expressions on clauses. In this case each condition is evaluated from top to bottom and the first to evaluate to true causes its statements to be executed and the when to terminate. In this case the when doesn't need to have an argument and the selection is completely general and can be used to replace complex nested ifs.

For example:

```
 when {
        a>=1 && a<=10 ->println("1 to 10")
        a<1 || a>5     ->println("not 1 to 10")
    }
```

This is the same as the previous range example and the first `println` is executed if a is in the range 1 to 10 and the second is printed if a is not in 1 to 10. As described earlier, the second condition is not a typing mistake.

Testing For Type

You can even use objects in a when, but in this case the test is for equality of reference, not type. That is, the clause that is executed is the one that has a reference to the same object.

For example:

```
when(obj1){
     obj2->println("same object")
     else->println("different object")
}
```

prints the message "same object" if obj1 and obj2 reference the same object, i.e. if obj1==obj2.

If you want to test for equality of type then you have to use the fact that you can use a general expression.

For example:

```
when(obj){
  is MyClass1 ->obj.doMethod()
 }
```

Nested if Versus when

Given the flexibility in specifying the condition within a when statement, you can often write a deeply nested if statement much more clearly using when. Take a simple situation with three products A, B and C. For A the discount is 0.1; for B costing less than $100 the discount is 0.05 and 0.08 otherwise; and for C the discount is 0.2. All other products have zero discount. First let's implement a nested if:

```
if (product == "A") {
      discount = 0.1
   } else if (product == "B") {
       if (cost < 100) {
           discount = 0.05
       } else {
           discount = 0.08
       }
   } else if (product == "C") {
       discount = 0.2
   } else {
       discount = 0.0
   }
```

Good luck with pairing up the brackets. I'm not claiming that this is the best way to nest conditions, just that it is typical.

You can see that this nested if is a decision tree and this can be "flattened" into a sequential decision process and implemented using a when.

Compare this nested if to the equivalent when:

```
when {
    product == "A" -> discount = 0.1
    product == "B" && cost < 100 -> discount = 0.05
    product == "B" -> discount = 0.08
    product == "C"->discount=0.2
    else -> discount=0.0
}
```

It is a simple list of the conditions needed for each discount. Although it isn't needed, it is clearer to write the second condition on product B as:

```
product==B && cost>=100 -> discount=0.08
```

This makes the condition that results in a discount of 0.08 completely clear and removes the dependence of the when on the order of the clauses.

It is a general principle that you should try to write conditions so that the order of the tests doesn't matter. This gives you protection from an innocent programmer accidentally changing the order of the conditions, while say adding to them, without realizing that it matters.

In most cases a when is preferable to a deeply nested if structure.

Using if & when As Expressions

One very important point about the if and the when statements is that they can both be used as expressions and they return the last value calculated. The only restriction is that an if or when statement used as an expression has to have an else part. For example:

```
var x=if (a>1) 1 else 0
```

or:

```
var x=when{
        a>0-> 1
      else-> 0}
```

If you call a function then the result will be the value of the function or unit if the function doesn't return a value.

The fact that you can use the if statement as an expression means that there is no need for a ternary operator as the if expression does exactly the same job. In Java you might write:

```
x=a>1 ? 1,0
```

which is exactly the same as the more readable Kotlin:

```
x= if(a>1) 1 else 0
```

The while Loop

Kotlin has only three loops – the `while`, `do while` and the `for`, but this is more than enough. Each of them works much as in other languages. Of the three, `for` is the most interesting, and we will meet it after considering `while` loops.

The `while` and `do while` loops are both conditional loops. The `while` has the condition at the start of the loop and the `do while` has it at the end.

For example:

```
while(x>0){
 do something
}
```

is a loop that will repeat while x is greater than zero, and:

```
do{
 do something
} while(x>0)
```

is also loop that will repeat while x is greater than zero.

What is the difference?

The answer is that if x is already zero or less when the loop starts the while loop will not be executed at all, but the `do while` loop will be executed once. This corresponds to the test for the `while` being at the start of the loop and for the `do while` at the end of the loop.

Put another way, a `while` loop can repeat zero or more times and a `do while` loop can repeat one or more times.

Nested Control With break & continue

While and `do while` are simple and easy to understand and if possible you should try to use them as they are. However, there are times when a problem is easier to solve by jumping out of a loop in the middle of the block of code rather than just at the start or the end. You can do this using the `break` statement.

The Kotlin `break` statement goes beyond what you might have encountered in other languages. At its simplest, `break` brings a loop to an end.

For example:

```
while(x>0){
  do something 1
 if(condition) break
  do something 2
}
```

In this case the loop will exit when the `if` statement's condition is true. When the loop exits via the `break` the instructions before the `break` will have been executed once more than the instructions after the break, i.e *do something 1* will execute one more time than *do something 2*.

The continue statement works like break, but it causes the loop to abandon the current iteration and start over. If the break statement is like a jump out of the loop to the instruction following, the continue is like a jump back to the start of the loop. For example:

```
while(x>0){
  do something 1
 if(condition) continue
  do something 2
}
```

In this case the loop moves on to the next iteration if the condition is true. This means that *do something 1* might be executed any number of times more often than *do something 2*. In fact, if the condition is always true, *do something 2* never gets executed.

Labels

The break and the continue are two of the three nested control statements that are present in Kotlin, the other being return. These are nested control statements because they can appear in a situation where they are nested within other control structures. You can, for example, place a break in the inner loop of a set of nested loops. Nested flow of control statements are more sophisticated than you might think.

First the shock news – Kotlin has labels.

In Kotlin you can assign a label to any expression. A label takes the form of an identifier ending in @ and all you have to do is place the label in front of the expression.

The good news is that statement labels aren't used for anything as dangerous as an unconstrained goto or other jump instruction. Instead they serve the purpose of identifying which of a set of nested constructs is being referred to. This works with the break and the continue simply enough, but its use with return is more complicated and depends on understanding inline functions, more of which in Chapter 11.

If you have a set of nested loops, break with a trailing label will break out of all the loops to the level of the loop with that label. That is, execution continues as if the labeled loop had terminated.

For example, consider:

```
var i = 0
var j = 0
while (i < 10) {
    i++
    while (j < 10) {
        j++
        print(i)
        print(",")
        println(j)
        if (j > 4) break
    }
}
```

In this case the inner loop breaks when j equals 5 and so you see i from 1 to 10 and j from 1 to 5. If we label the outer loop and use it in the break the behavior is different:

```
var i = 0
var j = 0
loop@ while (i < 10) {
    i++
    while (j < 10) {
        j++
        print(i)
        print(",")
        println(j)
        if (j > 4) break@loop
    }
}
```

As in the last example, the break is executed when j equals 5, but now it ends both the inner and outer loop and execution continues after the outer loop, i.e. the one labeled loop@.

The same idea applies to continue and return. For continue the situation is exactly the same as for break in that the loop that is restarted is the one labeled. Notice that this means that the inner loops terminate.

For example:

```
var i = 0
var j = 0
loop@ while (i < 10) {
    i++
    while (j < 10) {
        j - j + 1
        print("j=")
        println(j)
        if (j > 4) continue@loop
    }
    print("i=")
    println(i)
}
```

39

In this case the outer loop is intended to print a value for i and the inner loop prints a value for j, but because of the `continue@loop` the outer loop never prints the value of i. The reason is that the inner loop's `continue@loop` restarts the outer loop and hence aborts the inner loop. Restarting the outer loop means that its `print` statements are never executed.

Using `break` and `continue` with loops is sometimes convenient, but you should always consider what makes for easy-to-read code. There is a strong argument that `break` and `continue` only make sense in a very limited range of situations which apply more to `for` loops than to conditional loops.

The for Loop

The Kotlin `for` loop is both much simpler and more sophisticated than the standard Java or C `for` loop. It doesn't make use of the idea of a start value, a finish value, and an increment. Instead it is a simple iterator through a finite set of things. The good news is that where this is reducible to a traditional `for` loop with index, this is what the compiler does, so there is no loss of efficiency.

The general for loop is:

```
for(item in collection) {
 things to do
}
```

This, of course, leads us to the question of what sort of collections can be used in a for loop?

The simple answer is any object that has an iterator method that returns an object that has a `next` and a `hasNext` method.

For example, range expressions are iterable.

A range expression is created using the `rangeTo` function which is also usable as the infix operator `..` (two dots).

There is a range expression for each of the integral `IntRange`, `LongRange` and `CharRange` types. These are optimized in the sense that they are compiled to the traditional index-based `for` loop.

So, for example:

```
for(i in 1..10){
        println(i)
    }
```

prints 1 to 10 as you would expect. As `..` is just operator shorthand for the `rangeTo` function you can write this as:

```
for(i in 1.rangeTo(10) ){
        println(i)
    }
```

There are also `downTo` and `step` functions that can be used to modify the sequence. For example:

```
for(i in 10.downTo(1) ){
        println(i)
    }
```

prints 10 down to 1 and:

```
for(i in 10.downTo(1).step(2) ){
        println(i)
    }
```

prints 10,8,6,4,2.

As `downTo` and `step` are defined as operators these loops are usually written:

```
for(i in 10 downTo 1 ){
        println(i)
    }
```

and:

```
for(i in 10 downTo 1 step 2){
        println(i)
    }
```

Notice that `step` cannot be negative and so you have to control the direction of the loop using `downTo`, which essentially makes the step negative.

What about the most common form of for loop found in other languages such as Java?

For example, in Java you might write:

```
for(int i=0; i<10; i++){...
```

This loop generates index values of 0,1,2...9, but it doesn't generate the final value 10. This is a natural loop to use to index a complete array as the final value can be set to the size of the array and the index range is correct, i.e. an array of size 10 has elements a[0] to a[9].

In Kotlin, when working with array elements don't have to use a range at all for the index. You can simply write:

```
for(i in array.indices){..
```

This eliminates the most common reason for needing a loop that doesn't include its final value. However there are times when you still need one. That is, the standard Kotlin `for` loop:

```
for(i in 0..10){
        println(i)
    }
```

includes the final value of 10, but if you don't want it to, you can use the `until` function.

That is:

```kotlin
for(i in 0 until 10){
 println(i)
}
```

only prints 0, 1, 2.. 9

There is more to say about Kotlin for loops in the chapters on arrays and on collections. The important point about the `for` loop is that you can use any class that implements the Iterable Interface in a simple `for` loop, but if you want to use `step` the class has to be a range which also defines the `step` function.

Kotlin Control

The flow of control statements available in Kotlin are superficially similar to those found in Java, C/C++, C# and other similar languages. They are, however, significantly improved. The danger is that if you are more familiar with another language you will continue to write control statements that are essentially closer to that other language than idiomatic Kotlin.

It is important to keep in mind that Kotlin provides ways of writing control structures that are easier to understand and this should always be your number one goal, even before the goal of writing correct code!

If code is clear its incorrectness will be obvious.

If it is unclear then it is only correct until someone tries to change it.

Summary

- The Kotlin if is much like what you would find in other languages. You can have if, else and else if clauses.

- If nesting of if clauses becomes deep, try using the when statement. This also allows you to convert a nested structure into a "flat" set of mutually exclusive tests.

- A when can test for equality, general expressions, ranges, logical conditions, object equality and type.

- Both when and if can be used as expressions returning the last value computed.

- As an expression, if does away with the need for a ternary operator.

- The while loop executes zero or more time and the do while loop executes one or more times.

- The control break can be used to abort a loop – execution continues as if the loop had finished.

- Use continue to abort one iteration of a loop.

- Statements can be labeled and break and continue can use labels to abort outer loops and loop iterations.

- The for loop always takes the form of an iterator through a collection object.

- To construct the more familiar C/C++/Java for loop with an index, you can make use of range expressions.

Chapter 4

Arrays & Strings

Arrays and strings are so familiar that you might think you don't need to give them any attention. However, Kotlin has its own way of doing most things, including data structures.

The array and the string are the two most basic data structures – you almost can't write a program without using one of the two. Arrays in Kotlin are based on Java's array object, but the implementation is different enough to confuse. Similarly, the Kotlin string is essentially the same as the Java string, but with some interesting additions. In this chapter we look at Kotlon's treatment of these two fundamental data structures.

Many programmers are of the opinion that you shouldn't use a simple array unless performance is an issue. Instead you should use a more sophisticated data structure from the collection library, such as List or MutableList. These are not only more flexible but in theory less error-prone than the simple array. It doesn't make any real difference if you do adopt the "use a List in place of array" approach because the array is still the place where it all begins.

Arrays

Arrays in Kotlin aren't native objects, but instances of the `Array` class. This is a generic class, see Chapter 8 for a full account of Generics, and you can create arrays of any other type.

Creating an array is slightly different in Kotlin to Java in that you have to call a constructor or a factory function that makes the array. Kotlin arrays may be slightly different, but they are JVM Java arrays and work in exactly the same way under the cover.

The `arrayOf` function takes a list of values all of the same type and returns them as an array.

For example to create an array of three integers you would use:

```
var a=arrayOf(1,2,3)
```

The array type has `get` and `set` functions which accept an index, but these are also mapped to the [] operator and so you can write:

```
var b:Int=a[0]
a[0]=5
```

or:

```
var b:Int=a.get(0)
a.set(0,5)
```

You can create an array of any type in the same way.

For example:

```
var a=arrayOf(1.2,2.2,3.3)
```

creates an array of floats, and:

```
var a=arrayOf('a','b','c')
```

creates an array of chars. In each case, type inference is used to determine what `arrayOf` is of.

This is a completely general mechanism in that you really can use it to create an array of any type.

For example, suppose we have the following simple class, see Chapter 5:

```
class myClass(val v:Int) {
    var myProperty = v
}
```

then the function call:

```
var a=arrayOf(myClass(0),myClass(1),myClass(2))
```

creates an array of three instances of myClass.

If you want arrays of primitive types then it is more efficient to use one of:

byteArrayOf	booleanArrayOf
intArrayOf	charArrayOf
shortArrayOf	floatArrayOf
longArrayOf	doubleArrayOf

The objects created by these functions have the same methods as the array type, but they do not inherit from it, i.e. they are not subtypes of Array. They also create arrays of unboxed elements.

That is, if you create an array using:

```
var a=intArrayOf(1,2,3)
```

then the elements of the array are raw integers and not boxed integers, i.e. not Int objects. This is usually more efficient.

Larger Arrays

You can see that `arrayOf` is very useful, but defining arrays by specifying a list of values is very limited. For example, how can you create an array of 1000 integers?

In many other languages you would do this by creating an uninitialized array and then arrange to initialize it at some later time – usually via a `for` loop. Of course, in Kotlin you either have to initialize a variable or declare it to be nullable and so the casual approach of just creating an array of uninitialized array elements isn't going to work.

Kotlin provides two approaches.

The first is to use a factory function to create an array of nullable types all initialized to null. To do this you have to make use of the generic function:

```
arrayOfNulls<type>(size)
```

This creates an array as a nullable type and of the size specified.

For example:

```
var a= arrayOfNulls <Int>(1000)
```

creates an array of 1000 Ints all set to null.

You can assign any value to one of the elements, but if you try to use an element in an expression you either have to assign to another nullable or test to make sure that the element isn't null, i.e. you have to play by the rules for nullable types.

For example:

```
var a= arrayOfNulls <Int>(1000)
var b:Int=0
b=a[0]
```

generates a compile-time warning that b isn't a nullable type. Changing b's declaration to:

```
var b:Int?=0
```

makes it work.

A much better alternative in most cases is to initialize a non-nullable type. This can be done using the `Array` constructor which accepts a size parameter and a function to do the initialization:

```
Array(size, initializer)
```

The type of the array is determined by the type the initializer returns. The function, usually written as a lambda, is passed a single Int, the index, and the value it returns is stored in that element.

For example:

```
var a = Array(1000, { i -> i * 2 })
```

creates an array of 1000 Ints initialized so that a[i]=2*i. The initialization function can be as complicated as you like but the most common is:

```
var a = Array(1000, { 0 })
```

which zeros the array. Notice that the function simply returns zero and doesn't need the value of the parameter.

A more sophisticated example creates 1000 instances of an object:

```
var a = Array(1000, { i -> myClass(i) })
```

Limitations

If you are familiar with any language other than Java, there are some limitations of Kotlin arrays that you need to keep in mind. The first is that a Kotlin array is static in the sense that you cannot change its size once it has been declared. If you want a dynamic array that can change its size you need to use List and MutableList – see Chapter 9 on collections.

A second limitation is that Kotlin arrays are invariant. Exactly what this means is explained in Chapter 8, but essentially you cannot cast an array of one type of element to an array of another type, even if the element is a super class. That is, you cannot use:

```
var a = arrayOf(1,2,3,4)
var b:Array<Any>
b=a
```

This is what you might well expect, given that an array of Any can have elements of any type.

For example:

```
var b=Array<Any>(10,{0})
b[0]="mystring"
b[1]=1.1
println(b[0])
println(b[1])
println(b[2])
```

works perfectly and prints a string, a float and an integer. If you are working with an array of Any you clearly have to be careful to check the type of any element you are going to work with.

It is also worth noting that Kotlin has no array slicing facilities, i.e. the ability to specify a sub-array, that are found in languages such as Python. There is a good chance that these will be added in the future.

Array Processing

A very standard idiom is to use a `for` loop to process the elements stored in an array. The `for` loop was introduced in the Chapter 3 but it is worth describing the different ways in which an array and a `for` loop fit together.

The simplest array `for` loop is:

```
for(i in b.indices){
    println(b[i])
  }
```

In this case the `for` loop runs from 0 to size-1.

That is, it is equivalent to:

```
for(i in (0..b.size-1)){
    println(b[i])
  }
```

As well as the standard `for` loop, arrays also have `forEach` and `forEachIndexed` functions. Notice that these are not control structures that are part of the language, but array methods.

The `forEach` function accepts a function with a single parameter. The function is called repeatedly with the parameter set to each element of the array in turn. For example:

```
b.forEach({a->println(a)})
```

The `forEachIndexed` method works in the same way, but its function accepts two parameters, the element and the index.

For example;

```
b.forEachIndexed({a,i->println(a);println(i)})
```

Multidimensional Arrays

Creating multidimensional arrays is implemented in the same way as in most other modern languages. A 2-D array, for example, is just an array of arrays.

For example:

```
var a=arrayOf(arrayOf(1,2,3),arrayOf(4,5,6),arrayOf(7,8,9))
```

creates a 3 x 3 array. The array is a 1-D array of three elements in which each element is another 3-element array.

How do you write a for loop to scan through the elements? Easy, just use indices again:

```
for(i in a.indices){
        for(j in a[i].indices)
            println(a[i][j])
    }
```

There are, of course, many variations on how to create a multidimensional array. For example to create a 100 x 100 array you can use:

```
var b=Array(100, {Array(100,{0})})
```

which creates an array of 100 arrays of 100 Ints set to zero.

Whatever method of creating a multidimensional array you use, it is important not to fall into the trap of:

```
var col=arrayOf(1,2,3)
var b=arrayOf(col,col,col)
```

This appears to create a 3 x 3 array. It does, but the three columns are the same object so if you change b[0][0] you will find that b[1][0] and b[2][0] have been changed to the same value.

The array object has a very large number of methods which can be used to manipulate it. It has all of the Java methods and a few new ones. There are too many to go into the use of each one, but consult the documentation of the standard library before you start to write a function to do anything that might possibly be a common operation.

Strings

Kotlin strings are essentially Java strings with some extras. A string is much like an array of chars. You can create a string simply by assigning a string literal to it, for example:

```
var s="abc"
```

You can access the individual elements of the string using the [] operator which behaves as if the string was an array of char. Indexing in strings starts from zero just as for arrays.

For example:

```
var s="abcdef"
println(s[1].javaClass)
```

Here s[1] is 'b' and the print statement produces "char", its type.

Like Java, Kotlin strings are immutable and this means you cannot assign to an element.

That is:

```
s[2]='x'
```

will produce a compile-time error. Notice that the string being immutable doesn't mean that a variable referencing a string is immutable. If the variable is declared using val, then it is read-only and you cannot assign it a new string, but as long as it is declared as var you can. For example:

```
var s="abcdef"
s="xyz"
```

is perfectly OK.

String Processing

Operations with immutable strings generally involve taking sections from existing strings and putting them together to create a completely new string.

There are many string methods that allow you to extract part of a string and the concatenation operator + allows you to join them together.

The most often used string method is substring which comes in a large number of forms which allow you to specify the start and end of the substring you want. The version that is most idiomatic Kotlin, however, is:

```
substring(range)
```

where range specifies the start and end indices of the substring you want.

For example:

```
var s="abcdef"
println(s.substring(0..2))
```

prints abc.

Using substring and + you can write an expression that appears to change, say, the third element of the string:

```
var s="abcdef"
s=s.substring(0..1)+"x"+s.substring(3..s.length-1)
```

This works by extracting "ab" and "def" and putting them back together with "x" between them. Notice that this only looks as if the third element of the original string has changed. In fact what has happened is that a whole new string has been constructed and assigned to s.

The old string, assuming it hasn't any other variables referencing it, will eventually be garbage collected.

To convert this into a general expression for replacing the ith character all you need is:

```
s=s.substring(0..i-1)+"x"+ s.substring(i+1..s.length-1)
```

Of course you need to account for the special cases i=0 and i=length-1. Notice that x here is a string as we are concatenating strings.

Working in this way you can do anything with an immutable string that a mutable string would allow. The reason for using immutable strings is that they make memory allocation simpler as they have a fixed size. The downside is that any changes you need to make involve creating a new string and abandoning the old. This is generally efficient in time, but not in memory.

If you want a mutable string then you can use the Java `StringBuilder` class:

```
var s=StringBuilder("abcdef")
s[2]='x'
```

Notice that x has to be a char because `StringBuilder` is like an array of chars.

The StringBuilder allocates a char buffer that is slightly larger than the string needs and uses this extra space if more chars are added to the string at a later time. Once this space is used up the StringBuilder allocates more memory and this can be a slow process.

You can also create a StringBuilder with a specific initial capacity. There are also `insert` and `append` methods which can be used to insert and append additional text.

String Literals

Next we come to the interesting subject of Kotlin's string literals. There are two types - escaped and raw.

An escaped literal is what you are most likely to be familiar with. You can include escaped characters by placing a \ in front which changes the meaning of the character.

For example:

```
print("Hello World \n")
```

includes a newline code, rather than an n, at the end of the string.

The standard escaped characters in Kotlin are:

```
\t   tab
\b   backspace
\n   newline
\r   carriage return
\'   single quote
\"   double quote
\\   slash
\$   dollar
```

Notice that single quote, double quote, slash and dollar escapes have the effect of converting characters that by default have a special meaning to just ordinary characters.

The meaning of the dollar sign as a special character in Kotlin strings will be explained later.

You can also include any Unicode character found in in the BMP (Basic Multilingual Plane), i.e the first 65000 characters or so, using:

```
\uHHHH
```

where H is a hexadecimal integer.

For example:

```
var s = "\u016C"
```

stores the Latin Extended-A block capital letter U with breve, i.e. Ŭ

Note that Java, and hence Kotlin, does not support two word UTF-16 codes so you are restricted to the BMP and 16-bit codes.

The new raw string literal in Kotlin is designed to make entering longer and formatted text easier. A raw string literal is indicated by three double quotes. A raw string can contain no escape characters, but it can contain any character you can enter including control characters such as newline, etc. As the raw string is delimited by """ you can have a single double quote and a double double quote but not a triple double quote within a raw string. Also note that the raw string includes all of the characters between the delimiters, including any that the code editor might add in formatting your program.

For example:

```
var s="""Hello World"""
print(s)
```

just prints Hello World with no changes. However:

```
var s = """Hello
    World"""
    print(s)
```

as automatically formatted by IntelliJ, prints:

```
Hello
    World
```

You can include an initial and final newline by putting the """ on lines of their own:

```
var s = """
Hello
World
"""
```

String Templates

Perhaps the most useful new feature in Kotlin strings is the template. Put simply, you can include an expression that will be evaluated when the string is constructed and inserted into the string. An expression is indicated by a leading dollar sign followed by an expression in curly brackets. If the expression is a single variable then the curly brackets can be omitted.

So for example:

```
var s="Name $name and Address $address"
```

will insert the values of name and address into the string. Of course, the variables have to contain a string or have valid ToString methods that provide the appropriate text.

It is very important to understand that string templates are evaluated only once, i.e. when the string is constructed – the expressions are not live and will not be re-evaluated.

For example, consider the following:

```
var i = 1
var s = "The value of I is $i"
println(s)
i = 2
println(s)
```

Even though the value of i has changed the second println still prints:

```
The value of I is 1.
```

Compare this to:

```
var i = 1
println("The value of I is $i")
i = 2
println("The value of I is $i")
```

Now you see the correct value of I each time, i.e. it prints:

```
"The value of I is 1"
"The value of I is 2"
```

The reason, of course, is that there are two different string literals being used and each is constructed at the same time as the println it is used in. Putting a string template in a loop or a function ensures that it is constructed afresh each time it is used.

Using string templates within print statements is one way to achieve a more complex display. For example:

```
println("Name $name and Address $address")
```

The problem here is that string templates don't, yet, have any format control. That is, how can you print a value to say three decimal places? Using just Kotlin you can't, unless you write a function to do the job. However:

```
System.out.printf("The value of Pi is %.3f",pi)
```

prints 3.141, i.e. pi to three decimal places.

A slightly more Kotlin-oriented version of the same idea is to use Java's format string method:

```
println("The value of Pi is %.3f".format(pi))
```

Eventually no doubt Kotlin will acquire its own formatted templates, but for now we can fall back on Java.

You can use templates in both escaped and raw strings. In an escaped string you can enter a $ sign using \$. How can we enter a $ in a raw string?

The answer is obvious after a moment's thought. You can use an expression which returns a dollar sign as a literal. That is, to enter a $ into a raw string simply use:

```
"""this is a raw string $('$') with a dollar symbol"""
```

The number of functions available in the String class is huge and you can spend a great deal of time exploring them all. In general, if you want to do something check the documentation for a function that can do the job for you or can help with the problem. In particular, remember that Kotlin supports Java's regular expressions, which can solve many problems in one go.

Summary

- Kotlin arrays are compatible with Java arrays and are instances of the `Array` class.

- Arrays are created using either factory methods such as `arrayOf` or using the constructor.

- The `arrayOf` factory method can be used to create short arrays of literal data.

- The primitive type `ArrayOf` factory method can be used to create pure Java arrays.

- To create a large array use either `arrayOfNulls`<*type*>(*size*) or the constructor `Array`(*size*, *initializer*) where *initializer* is a function that returns the value for each element.

- There are many ways of processing arrays using a `for` loop. Use the indices range or the `forEach` method.

- Multidimensional arrays are constructed as arrays of arrays in the usual way.

- Kotlin strings are compatible with Java strings. They are immutable and fixed in size.

- String processing is generally a matter of taking strings apart using `substring` or similar functions and then putting them back together using string concatenation.

- If you need a mutable dynamic string then you have to fallback to using the Java StringBuilder.

- String literals come in two types – escaped and raw.

- String templates let you easily build strings that include the values of variables.

Chapter 5

The Class And The Object

Kotlin is a class-based, object-oriented language and it works in a way that is compatible with Java objects. This doesn't mean that Kotlin does classes in exactly the same way as Java or any other language. In fact, part of the problem in getting to grips with Kotlin classes is that initially they look as if they are just like Java classes – but they aren't.

They may be compatible with Java classes, but Kotlin offers some significant novel approaches to objects.

Classes

Despite initial appearances, Kotlin is a full object-oriented language. Even though you can have functions at the package level these are in fact bundled up into methods of a default class.

In Kotlin everything is an object.

Kotlin is fairly traditional in its approach to objects. It restricts inheritance to single inheritance and it supports interfaces with some inherited implementation to get around this restriction. It is also strongly-typed, despite managing to make code look as if type isn't important by using type inference.

The first big shock is how easy it is to create a class and an instance:

```
class MyClass
var myObject=MyClass()
```

Notice that you don't need to use new, just use the class name as if it was a function, which of course it is, the constructor. A class doesn't even need a body, although you can add a pair of empty curly brackets if you want to:

```
class MyClass{}
var myObject=MyClass()
```

You can include a type specifier for clarity:

```
var myObject:MyClass=MyClass()
```

but this isn't the Kotlin idiom as type inference easily supplies the type.

A Kotlin class can have properties and methods, i.e. properties that are functions. Both properties and methods are accessed in the usual way using the dot notation.

For example if myMethod is a method that is defined in MyClass you can write:

```
var myObject=MyClass()
myObject.myMethod()
```

You can access properties in the same way, although it is worth keeping in mind that all Kotlin properties make use of getter and setter functions which are automatically generated if you do not supply them. That is, Kotlin classes do not have fields, i.e. member variables that are directly accessible outside of the class.

The Primary Constructor

A class often has multiple constructors to allow it to be customized in different ways. In other languages all of the constructors are generally treated as being of equal importance – with the possible exception of a single parameterless construction which can be called by the system to create a default instance. More importantly, they are all defined in the same way as methods within the body of the class declaration. This is not true in Kotlin.

In Kotlin a class can have one primary constructor and as many secondary constructors as you like, and the primary constructor seems to be special in some way.

The primary constructor can be a puzzle to programmers familiar with Java and other languages where constructors are simply methods that have the same name as the class.

Kotlin does away with the redundancy of having to keep on stating the class name within the class definition. In Kotlin the class declaration is also the declaration of the primary constructor, and you can include parameters if you want to:

```
class MyClass(count:Int=0)
```

The primary constructor is convenient but it is limited.

You can't place any instructions in the primary constructor because it doesn't have a method body. That is, you can't write something like:

```
class MyClass(count:Int){
    if(count<0) count=0;
}
```

The primary constructor has no method body and the body of the class declaration is for writing class members and secondary constructors. It is not the method body of the primary constructor, even though it might at first sight be mistaken for one.

That is, the primary constructor is simply a list of parameters that can be passed when the class is instantiated.

The question is, what can you do with these parameters if the primary constructor has no method body?

The most you can do is to use the primary constructor's parameters in property initializers:

```kotlin
class MyClass(count:Int){
    val max=count;
    }
```

Notice that max is a property of MyClass and nothing to do with the primary constructor, except that it uses a parameter as an initializer.

This is such a common idiom that Kotlin provides a way to link properties and the parameters in the primary constructor automatically.

If you specify var or val in front of a parameter then it is converted into a read/write or read-only property, complete with initializers.

For example:

```kotlin
class MyClass(var count:Int=0)
```

has a read/write property called count initially set to zero.

This idiom makes creating data-only classes, what would be called structs or records in other languages, easy.

For example:

```kotlin
class Person(val Name:String,var Address:String)
```

creates a class with a Name and an Address property. Kotlin goes a little further than this in its support of data representation – see Data Classes in Chapter 12.

At the moment it looks as if the primary constructor is limited, but see Initializer Blocks later in this chapter. Adding an initializer block provides a way of executing some code independently of which constructor is called, and this includes the primary constructor.

Secondary Constructors

For a great many classes a primary constructor is all that is needed because initializing an instance comes down to creating and initializing some properties.

If your class needs more initialization than this, or if you need to allow alternative forms of initialization, then you need to define secondary constructors.

These are methods prefixed by the keyword constructor – you don't have to give them names as Kotlin understands constructors. You can also put the keyword `constructor` in front of the primary constructor if you want to, and you have to if you put any access specifier or annotation on the line.

Also notice that you don't have to have an explicit primary constructor - if you don't want one just omit the () and parameters after the class name. Kotlin automatically creates a parameterless primary constructor for you.

For example:

```
class MyClass{
        constructor(Name:String){
        println(Name)
    }
}
```

is a class without an explicit primary constructor, and with a single secondary constructor that accepts a single string.

You can have multiple overloaded constructors and the one that matches the signature of the call will be used.

Once you have defined a primary constructor then the secondary constructors have to call it using:

`this(parameters)`

and you do have to supply any parameters that don't have defaults.

For for example:

```
class MyClass{var Name:String=""){
        constructor(Name: String) {
            println(Name)
        }
        constructor(Name:String,Address:String):this(Name){
            println(Name)
        }
}
```

If a secondary constructor delegates to another constructor by calling it, then it doesn't have to call the primary, but the other constructor does.

What all this comes down to is that the primary constructor has to be called somehow.

Also notice that the trick of including `var` and `val` to automatically create properties only works with the primary constructor.

Initializer Blocks

There is one more twist in the Kotlin class declaration. You can define initializer blocks.

These are blocks of code within the class declaration that are run before the constructor. Even though they run before the constructor the parameters passed to the constructor are available to them – they act like code inserted into the start of the constructor.

In Kotlin all initialization occurs in the order the code is listed, and before the constructor is run, but with the constructor parameters fully defined.

That is, the initializer really does look like a block of code that is inserted into the very start of every constructor.

For example:

```
class MyClass(Name:String) {
        init {
            println(Name)
        }
}
var myObject = MyClass("Mickey Mouse")
```

The init block runs before the constructor but Name is set to "Mickey Mouse". This order of execution can be confusing at first, but it is simple, logical and, as long as you understand it, shouldn't cause any errors.

You can have as many init blocks and as many constructors as you need and you don't need to define an explicit primary constructor.

Constructor Chaos?

At this point you might be confused as to how all these facilities fit together – it seems we have too many ways of defining what can happen when an instance is created. The important thing to note about the initializer is that it runs as if it was the initial code for each of the constructors – hence it is the ideal way to carry out anything that has to happen irrespective of which constructor is used.

When creating a class you have a number of different levels of constructor complexity you can adopt:

1) The simplest is just to use a primary constructor to create a class with properties corresponding to the parameters used.

2) Next you can define an initialization block which defines what happens when any constructor, including the primary constructor, is called.

3) You can define any number of overloaded constructors that allow the user to create instances in different ways.

4) Finally you can add code to each of the overloaded constructors that defines the unique actions that need to be performed when that particular constructor is used.

In most cases all you need is a primary constructor and possibly an initializer block.

Class Members – Methods & Properties

Of course, as well as constructors and init blocks, a class can have properties and methods, and so far we haven't said much about them,

There isn't much to say about methods – you simply define a function within a class and call it using the usual dot notation.

There are a few things to say about properties, however. Properties can be read/write or read-only as declared using var or val.

Properties declared using var have default getters and setters and those declared using val have only a getter i.e. val properties are read-only.

All properties are accessed via getter/setter functions and, unlike in Java, you don't have to explicitly create them – the compiler will do the job for you. It will also automatically put get or set in front of the property's name so that you can use Java properties implemented in this way without having to modify property names.

Notice that a class cannot have a simple field, i.e. a variable that is directly accessible without the use of a getter or setter. All variables defined within a class declaration are properties.

If you want a custom getter or setter you simply define them after the property declaration. The only thing you have to remember is that the property has a default backing field which can be accessed using the identifier field. This means that within the getter/setter you refer to the property value as field.

For example:

```
class MyClass(Name: String) {
    var myProp: Int = 1
        set(value) {
            if (value > 0) {
                field = value
            }
        }
        get() = field
    }
```

In this case the setter will only change the value of the property if it is positive.

Also notice that, unlike in languages such as Java, you don't have to call the getters and setters. You simply assign and make use of the property and the getter/setter is called as needed.

For example:

```
var myObject = MyClass("Mickey Mouse")
myObject.myProp = 3
println(myObject.myProp)
```

To be clear, the assignment to myProp calls the setter, and the use of myProp in the `println` calls the getter.

If you want to call Java code then you can use getter/setter Java properties as if they were Kotlin properties, i.e. without putting `get` or `set` into the property name or calling a function. If you want to call a Kotlin method from Java you simply use the corresponding get*Property* and set*Property* functions.

Behind the scenes, Kotlin uses the same code to create getter/setter properties as Java.

If you want to have your own backing variable you can simply declare one and use it:

```
class MyClass(Name: String) {
 private var myBacking:Int=0
 var myProp: Int
     set(value) {
                  if (value > 0) {
                      myBacking = value
                  }
             }
     get() = myBacking
 init {
         println(Name)
       }
}
```

Notice that in this case you can't initialize the property because it doesn't have a default backing variable. Instead you have to initialize the backing variable itself.

Late Initialized Properties

Much of this chapter has been about setting up and initializing properties. If the property is a non-null type then it has to be initialized in the constructor code. However, there are case where the property is more correctly initialized by some other function.

You can deal with this by initializing the property to a default value, or you can use a nullable type and have to deal with null checks from then, on or you can mark the property with `lateinit`. This only works for `var` non-null, non-primitive properties defined in the body of the class. The property can remain undefined for as long as you like, but if you try to access it before it is initialized you will generate an exception. For example:

```
class MyClass {
        lateinit var myMessage: String
        fun setMessage() {
            myMessage = "Message of the day"
        }
    }
```

In this case it is supposed that the `setMessage` function will be called before the property is used. If you do use it uninitialized:

```
var myObject = MyClass()
println(myObject.myMessage)
```

then you will see the error message:

```
Exception in thread "main"
kotlin. UninitializedPropertyAccessException: etc..
```

However if you do initialize it:

```
var myObject = MyClass()
myObject.setMessage()
println(myObject.myMessage)
```

everything works.

Inner Classes

Classes can have functions and properties as members, and they can also have other classes. A nested class is defined within another class. It is local to the containing or outer class in that it isn't visible outside of the containing class.

For example, `MyNestedClass` is local to `MyClassA`:

```
class MyClassA {
    class MyNestedClass {
        fun myInnerMethod() {
            println("myMethod")
        }    }    fun myOuterMethod() {
        var myNestedObject = MyNestedClass()
        myNestedObject.myInnerMethod()
    }
}
```

It can be used by methods inside `MyClassA`, but it is inaccessible from anywhere else.

By default nested classes cannot access the members of the outer class.

That is, if you try:

```
class MyClassA {
    var myString:String="Hello World"
     class MyNestedClass {
        fun myInnerMethod() {
            println(myString)
        }
      }
}
```

you will find that `myString` is unresolved and there is an error.

However, if you mark the nested class as `inner` then it can access the outer class's members. That is, with the addition of inner, `myInnerMethod` can now access `myString` in the outer class:

```
class MyClassA {
    var myString:String="Hello World"
    inner class MyInnerClass {
        fun myInnerMethod() {
            println(myString)
        }
    }
}
```

Inner classes are useful if you need to define classes that are useful to another class but not more generally useful. If you need to instantiate a lot of inner class objects then it makes sense. However, if you only need a single instance then using a Kotlin object makes better sense as you don't have to declare a class first.

The Object Singleton

Given that Kotlin is a class-based, object-oriented, language, if you want to create an object you first create a class and then use it to create instances of the object. The class is the blueprint for the object and by calling the constructor you can create as many instances of the object as you like.

This is usually what you want to do, but occasionally there is a need for just one instance of an object and in this case having to create a class seems like a roundabout way to work. Many languages allow you to create an object directly, without the use of a class, and Kotlin allows you to do this.

You can declare an object using very similar syntax to declaring a class. For example:

```
object myObject {
    fun say(message: String) {
        println(message)
    }
}
```

creates an object instance called `myObject` with a single `say` method. Directly following this declaration, you can call the method and there is no need to instantiate the object – indeed you can't as there is no class and no constructor. You use the object in the same way as you would any object:

`myObject.say("Hello World")`

There are some restrictions to be aware of. In particular, an object declaration cannot appear inside a function, including main. They can appear as part of an object or class declaration. You cannot declare an object in an inner class, however. The object declaration is a perfect way to implement the singleton pattern as, without a constructor, there can only be one instance.

Class Variations

As well as being useful in creating singletons, you can also use object declarations as a way of creating a slight variation on an existing class without having to go to the trouble of deriving a subclass.

All you have to do is include the class that you want to base your object on in the declaration:

```
object myObject:myClass() {
    fun say(message: String) {
        println(message)
    }
}
```

In this case `myObject` inherits all of the methods and properties defined in `myClass`. You can now add methods and properties to `myObject` and you can override the inherited methods and properties.

An object can also implement an interface.

Inheritance is described in full detail in the next chapter, but for this to work `myClass` has to be open and you have to use the `override` keyword on any method or property you redefine.

This is a very good way of creating ad-hoc objects without having to implement a full inheritance hierarchy. In some projects this fits with what you are trying to do; in others it is simply bad design.

Static Members & Companion Objects

If you know your Java, or almost any object-oriented language, you might be wondering where static methods and properties are in Kotlin?

In Java you can define a method as `static`:

```
class myClass{
  public static String myMethod() {
        return "Hello World";
  }
}
```

The `static` qualifier means you can now call the method as if it was a method of the class, i.e.

```
myClass.myMethod()
```

The purpose of static methods is to provide utility methods that don't depend on the particular instance of the class, or to provide utility methods that behave as if they were defined on a singleton.

Kotlin doesn't support static members. That is, you cannot define a method or property that belongs to the class. What you can do instead is create a companion object inside the class.

This might seem like a strange idea at first; but when you declare a static method you are treating the class as if it was an object in its own right. A companion object has the same name as the class and therefore any methods that you give it look like static methods. To declare a companion object all you have to do is use the keyword `companion` in front of the object's declaration. Of course, to be a companion it has to be declared within a class.

For example:

```
class myClass {
    companion object {
        fun myMethod() {
            println("Hello World")
        }
    }
}
```

defines a companion object for `myClass` with a single method, `myMethod`, which can be called using:

```
myClass.myMethod()
```

Notice that as objects cannot be local, neither can a companion object, and so the class has to be declared at the top level and not within a function, say.

You can access the companion variable as a complete object using the default name `Companion` or a custom name.

For example:

```
companion object myCompanion ...
```

and you can call `myMethod` using:

```
myClass.Companion.myMethod()
```

if you haven't assigned a custom object name.

Notice that while the companion object looks like a set of static members, it is a real object and can be used like a singleton object. For example, it can inherit from another class, it can be passed as a parameter, and it can implement interfaces.

This is an interesting new feature and it raises the idea of static members to another level. It provides a way to provide class-related utility functions as part of the class. The documentation advises that you should use package level functions in preference to objects, but notice that this approach doesn't allow you to associate functions with a particular class.

Object Expressions

The ability to create single instances of an object is very useful, but often it is more convenient to use the object at once without the bother of giving it a name or a long and permanent life. For example, if a function accepts an object as a parameter, then going to the trouble of creating a class with modifications and an instance is far too much work. Even declaring and customizing a top-level object complete with a name is more work than the problem warrants, and the object exists for the lifetime of the program.

Put simply, sometimes all we want is an anonymous object that is a slight modification of an existing class and which will have a relatively short life.

In Java the solution is to use an anonymous inner class.

In Kotlin the solution is to use an object expression.

The way to think about an object expression is that it is an expression which is evaluated at the point in the program at which it occurs and which evaluates to an object. Unlike an object declaration, which cannot be local, an object expression has to be local.

Finding an example of using an object expression that is simple isn't easy because the most common usage is to pass an object to a Java function – usually an event handler.

Although Kotlin has its own timer object, we can make use of the Swing timer, the constructor of which takes an integer delay in milliseconds, and an instance of `ActionListener`.

`ActionListener` is an interface which has a single `actionPerformed` method, which has to be defined to handle the timer interrupt. If you don't know about interfaces, they are covered in the next chapter. The important point is that we are creating an object directly from a class or interface definition.

We can use the Swing timer by adding an import:

```
import javax.swing.Timer
```

To create an instance of `Timer` we have to supply the `ActionListener` object and, as it will only be used by the timer an object expression is the obvious way to do the job;

```
var timer = Timer(1000, object : java.awt.event.ActionListener {
    override fun actionPerformed(e:java.awt.event.ActionEvent?) {
        println("Action Performed")
    }
})
```

If you are using IntelliJ you can use it to automatically generate the override. Notice that this has to be inside a function, for example main, for it to work.

If you now start the timer and put the program into an infinite loop to keep it running, you will see the message printed every second:

```
timer.start()
while(true){}
```

Notice that the only difference between an object declaration and an object expression is that it is used as an expression, i.e. it is assigned to a variable or passed as a parameter.

If you want to, you can store the result of an object expression in a variable:

```
val action=object :java.awt.event.ActionListener {
    override fun actionPerformed(e:java.awt.event.ActionEvent?) {
        println("Action Performed")
    }
}
```

and then this can be passed to the timer constructor:

```
var timer = Timer(1000,action)
timer.start()
while (true) {}
```

An object expression can inherit from one class and any number of interfaces. You can use any variables that are in scope when the expression is evaluated, i.e. local and global variables accessible in the function at the point the expression is being evaluated. Java inner classes, on the other hand, can only access variables that have been declared final.

The only restriction is that, if you return an object expression as the result of a function, it has the type of its super class and any members you have added are not accessible.

The documentation makes a point of emphasizing the differences between an object declaration and an object expression, but if you understand the difference between a general expression and declaration these should be obvious.

Object expressions are evaluated when they are used, i.e. when they are executed in the flow of control. By contrast, object declarations are evaluated lazily, i.e only when the object they declare is needed. A companion object can only be a declaration and it is initialized when its class is loaded.

Summary

- Every class has a primary constructor, even if it is just the default parameterless constructor provided by the system

- The primary constructor is just a declaration of parameters that can be used when an instance is created.

- You can use the parameters within the properties and methods defined in the class definition.

- Usually the parameters in the primary constructor are used to automatically create properties using `var` or `val`.

- If you want to do more in the constructor, or have overloaded constructors, you need to define secondary constructors.

- Secondary constructors have a method body and can execute code.

- A secondary constructor always has to call the primary constructor using the `this(`*parameters*`)` statement.

- A class can also have any number of initializer blocks which are executed after the constructor is called, but before any constructor body is executed.

Chapter 6

Inheritance

Inheritance was once the whole point of object-oriented programming. It was the big advantage and it promised easy code reuse. The reality wasn't so good, but it is still amazingly valuable as long as you use it correctly. Kotlin has facilities to help you control and work with both inheritance and an alternative, composition.

If you have a class then you can use this to create as many instances of the object that the class defines as you like. This is the whole point of using a class to define an object. After discovering how to create objects in the previous chapter, we are now going to look at how classes can be used in more sophisticated ways.

Copy & Paste Versus Inheritance

If you want to create a class that is very similar to a class that you already have, then the primitive way of doing the job is to simply copy the code from the base or super class, and paste to create the derived or sub class. Copy and paste inheritance is simple but if you make any changes to the base class these are not reflected in the sub class unless you repeat the copy and paste and the modifications you made.

To overcome this problem, the mechanism of inheritance was invented. You can give a new class all of the members of an existing class by making it inherit from the existing class. This means you can have code reuse without copy and paste, and the proposed advantage of this is that any changes to the super class are automatically communicated to the sub class.

This one big advantage has proved over the years to be a two-edged sword. The problem is often called "brittle base classes". If a base class isn't specifically designed to be used in an inheritance chain, small changes to the way it works can break most or all of the classes that are derived from it.

When a class is used as a base class it changes its importance. Imagine you are working on refactoring a class that isn't used as a base class. You are fairly free to do to it whatever you like as long as the class works. Now change it into a base class for hundreds of other derived classes. Any change that you make to it might just have an important effect on any of the derived classes and you just have to trust that everything is OK.

You can improve the safety of inheritance by controlling what is visible outside of a class. Roughly speaking, the idea is that you don't allow the inner workings of the class to leak out. Derived classes can only rely on what the base class does, and not how it does it. If all this is true then you can refactor the base class to your heart's content, safe in the knowledge that, as long as the result does the same job, the derived classes will be unaffected. All this is possible, but it does require some extra thought and some extra work.

When languages such as Java, were invented the enthusiasm for object-oriented programming was overwhelming and the idea was embraced completely. Today, Kotlin takes a more cautious approach to inheritance and provides as much protection against the pitfalls as it possibly can.

As a result Kotlin's object-oriented features are very similar to Java's but they differ in many small but important ways.

Inheritance

Kotlin classes support single inheritance. This means any class can inherit all of the members of one single class. Of course that single class might have inherited from another single class so resulting in a chain of inheritance. To indicate which class is the super class you simply write its name after a colon in the class declaration. For example:

```
class myClass:mySuperClass{...
```

If you don't specify a `SuperClass` then the default class is `Any` which is the fundamental class in Kotlin that all other classes are derived from.

In Java any class that you define can be used as a superclass unless you mark it as final – in which case it is not eligible to be used to create a derived class.

The big difference with Kotlin is that all classes are considered as final, i.e. cannot be inherited from, unless otherwise stated. This is the opposite of most languages which expect the programmer to explicitly indicate a class not intended to act as a base class.

To mark a class as suitable for inheritance you have to add the keyword `open` to its declaration.

```
open myClass {...
```

The thinking behind this is that inheritance is too serious a matter to enter into without designing for it. If you create a class then the default is that it will not be used as the base class for anything else. It is what it is, and it will not lead to a set of other derived classes. So if you want to use a class as a base class then you need to add `open` to its declaration, which it is hoped might make you think hard about the design of the class.

Inheritance is easy to implement but difficult to manage.

Inherited Constructors

Inheritance is easy, but you have to deal with the problem that the base class needs to be constructed before your derived class can add its extras and its modifications. You have to arrange to call the base class's constructor and this is something you have to do, even if the base class appears not to have an explicit constructor.

Due to the use of primary and secondary constructors, the rules for calling inherited constructors can seem quite complicated, but they are very logical. The key ideas are that the primary constructor of the base class always has to be called, and how this happens depends on whether or not the derived class also has an explicit primary constructor.

If a class has a primary constructor then all of the secondary constructors have to call it. This means that if the derived class has a primary constructor, then it has to call the base class's primary constructor if it has one, or a secondary constructor, which calls the base class's primary, if it doesn't. This ensures that any constructor in the derived class always eventually calls the base class's primary constructor.

If the derived class doesn't have an explicit primary constructor, then it is down to each of the secondary constructors to call one of the base class's constructors using the super keyword. Once again this will call the base class's primary constructor.

You can now see that the rule is that any secondary constructor in the derived class either has to call its own primary constructor, i.e. this() or, if there isn't a primary constructor, one of the super classes constructors, i.e. super().

Which particular secondary constructor is called depends on the signature of the parameters.

Let's see how this works. For example:

```
open class MyClassA {}
class MyClassB: MyClassA() {}
```

In this case the base class doesn't have any constructors and so the system creates a default parameterless constructor which the derived class calls from its primary constructor. No explicit primary constructor is needed because the default parameterless one will do.

If the base class has a primary constructor then it has to be called with appropriate parameter values:

```kotlin
open class MyClassA(name:String) {}
class MyClassB: MyClassA("Mickey Mouse") {}
```

If both classes have primary constructors and the derived class has a secondary constructor then it has to call the derived class's secondary constructor, which in turn calls the base class's primary constructor:

```kotlin
open class MyClassA(name: String) {}
class MyClassB(name:String): MyClassA(name) {
    constructor(name: String, telephone: String): this(name) {
        println("Hello")
    }
}
```

If the derived class doesn't have a primary constructor then the secondary constructors have to call a base class constructor for themselves.

For example:

```kotlin
open class MyClassA(name: String) {
    constructor(name: String, address: String): this(name) {
            println(name)
    }
}
class MyClassB:MyClassA {
 constructor(name: String, telephone: String): super(name,"street"){
            println("Hello")
 }
}
```

In this case the secondary constructor of the derived class calls super because there is no derived primary to call. This in turn causes the base class constructor to call the base class primary constructor if there is one. The derived class can also call the base class primary constructor directly using the correct signature. The secondary constructor can also call another constructor as long as it eventually results in the base or derived class primary constructor being called.

Interfaces

Although Kotlin is single inheritance, it also supports interfaces which, in most modern languages, provide a way to implement multiple inheritance in a supposedly safe way. Interfaces in Kotlin are similar to those in Java 8, but if you know "classical" interfaces you might be surprised at how close to a class a Kotlin interface is.

The original idea of an interface was that it would provide a specification of the methods that a class had to implement, but it would provide no implementation. This provides some of the security of inheritance, without the risk of inheriting methods that weren't appropriate for the derived class. The interface forced the programmer to implement all of the methods it declared from scratch, thus ensuring that they were all perfectly suited to the derived class. A programmer using the derived class could be confident that it had used of all of the methods declared in the interface.

For example, an interface called `Printable` could declare `print` and `println` methods for an object. Any object that implemented the `Printable` interface would be safe to call `print` or `println` on. An interface gives you a specification of what methods a class that implements it supports. However, it is very tedious to have to re-implement most of the methods defined in the interface because they often don't vary much in what they have to do. In short, interfaces often cause the programmer to go back to copy and paste inheritance.

As a result interfaces have tended to evolve into something that looks increasingly like class-based inheritance. That is, they come with code that is inherited. This has resulted in the idea that there are two types of method in an interface – a declaration without a code body, usually called abstract, and a fully implemented method.

A Kotlin interface can have abstract and implemented methods and implemented properties, but without backing fields.

Of course, interfaces aren't classes and can't have constructors and they can't have `init` blocks. This limits the complexity of the implementation of an interface to just a collection of basic methods that behave as if they had been copied and pasted into the class.

To create an interface you simply proceed as for a class but use the keyword `interface`.

For example:

```
interface A{
    fun myFunc1()
    fun myFunc2(){
        println("myFunc1")
    }
}
```

This defines an interface with two methods – `myFunc1` which is virtual, i.e. no implementation; and `myFunc2`; which is fully implemented. Notice that you don't have to use the keyword `open` to allow inheritance. The only purpose an interface serves is to be inherited and so they are open by default as are all of the functions and properties they define.

When a class inherits or implements an interface it gains all of the implemented methods and it has to implement any of the methods that are not implemented. Notice that implementing the virtual methods is not optional and the program won't compile until all interface methods are fully implemented. As properties in Kotlin are implemented as getter and setter methods, they are more or less the same as methods. You can declare a property in an interface and it can be abstract. In this case the class that implements the interface has to provide the property including any getter/setters. Alternatively you can implement its getter/setter methods in the interface but these cannot reference a backing variable. What this means is that either the inheriting class has to implement the method using a backing variable or the property has to implement get and set that use values generated by expressions or other functions.

For example:

```
interface A{
    val myprop:Double
    get()=random()
}
```

Note: random is provided by a Java library function so you will need to add import java.lang.Math.random

Conflicts

The classical use of an interface is to provide a set of unimplemented function and property definitions that a class can inherit and implement. The sole use of classical interfaces is to govern what methods and properties you can rely on existing in a class.

The more modern version of the concept of an interface allows you to define some inheritable implementations. This is often more efficient but, as a class can inherit in multiple ways from different interfaces, it can cause problems with multiple definitions of the same method or property.

This is one of the reasons why multiple inheritance, as supported in C++ say, is generally thought not to be a good idea. If a class can inherit from multiple base classes, the set of methods that are inherited might contain multiple definitions of what is supposed to be a single method. In this case we need rules that resolve such conflicts.

If a class implements two interfaces that define the same method, then the class has to override the method and provide its own implementation. In other words, clashes have to be resolved by redefining the method.

Of course, the new method can call one of the Interface methods. To do this use the call:

```
super<interface>.method()
```

where interface is the name of the interface and method is the name of the method you want to call. This mechanism is general and you can call any interface method in this way.

Overriding

One of the basic things that you do with inherited methods and properties is to override them by providing the class's own implementation.

In Kotlin you have to declare a method as open if it can be overridden because by default methods cannot be overridden. This again is an attempt to not accidentally fall into the complexities of inheritance without being aware of them. By default inherited methods cannot be overridden, i.e. redefined. You don't have to override a method marked as open, it is optional, but if you do, you have to mark the overriding method as override.

For example:

```kotlin
open class MyClassA(name: String) {
    open fun myFunc1() {
        println("myFunc1")
    }
}
class MyClassB(name:String):MyClassA(name){
    override fun myFunc1(){
        println("My New function")
    }
}
```

In this case an instance of MyClassB will have the version of the method that prints "My New function". If you miss out open or override the compiler will point this out.

You can override properties in the same way, the overridable property is marked open and the overriding property as override. The types have to be compatible, but you can completely redefine the property otherwise with new getter/setter and initialization. You can override a val with a var property, but not the other way round.

When overriding method implementation in an interface you have to use the override keyword, just as for a class.

By default an overridden method is open and can be overridden in a subsequent derived class. If you want to stop this, all you have to do is use the final keyword:

```kotlin
class MyClassB(name:String):MyClassA(name){
    final override fun myFunc1(){
        println("My New function")
    }
}
```

Abstract Classes

Classes and interfaces should be enough to tackle any inheritance-based design, but for largely historical reasons we also have abstract classes and methods.

An abstract class has abstract methods that are not implemented. You don't have to use the `abstract` modifier to create an abstract class. If you don't define some members then the class is inferred to be abstract. However, if you want to override a non-abstract inherited method with an abstract one, you do need to use the `abstract` modifier, but this isn't a common requirement.

Of course, you can't create an instance of an abstract class because it isn't complete. The only thing you can do with an abstract class is inherit it.

That is, an abstract class only exists to act as a base class. If a derived class implements all of the abstract methods then it can be instantiated.

Isn't an abstract class just another way of creating an interface?

The answer is "yes and no".

A class that has nothing but abstract methods looks a lot like an interface. Remember, however, that you can only inherit from one class, but you can choose to implement many interfaces. This means that interfaces can be set up to act like definitions of abilities that classes have to have. Abstract classes are used to define more fully what a class is, rather than just provide a set of abilities.

A class is also more general than an interface and an abstract class can have all of the things that a non-abstract class can – constructors, methods and properties backed by variables.

An abstract class is used within a standard class inheritance scheme where some of the methods or properties are so class specific that creating a derived class demands that they be re-implemented. You can think of the abstract methods defining the variation of the base class that the derived class implements.

For example, the much overworked example of classes that represent animals might have an abstract `makeSound` method which has to be implemented by any derived class – a dog goes woof, a cat meows and a mouse squeaks. Here the sounds define the derived class and so `makeSound` is abstract so as to force inheriting classes to implement their own version.

Delegation

As if classes, interfaces and abstract classes weren't enough ways to handle inheritance, Kotlin also supports delegation. In its most general form, delegation simply means creating an instance of a class within another class and then using its methods to implement the containing class's methods. This is supposed to be a safer form of "inheritance" and you will hear the saying "prefer composition to inheritance".

Composition is where one object acquires the methods of another by simply containing an instance of the object. Calls to the methods of the contained object are simply passed on to it by the containing object - a sort of delegation.

This is simple and direct, but manually creating all of the methods needed to redirect calls to the object that does all of the work is tedious and error prone.

For example, suppose we have a `Printer` class that prints some messages. We could use inheritance to give a derived class the same methods. Alternatively we could achieve the same result by creating an instance of the `Printer` class within our derived class.

That is, given the class:

```
class Printer{
    fun myFunc(mess: String) {
        println(mess)
    }
}
```

You can use manual delegation to implement a "derived" class which has the same myFunc method implemented class quite simply by the existing `Printer`:

```
class MyClass{
 var printerObject=Printer()
 fun myFunc(mess:String){
     printerObject.myFunc(mess)
 }
}
```

You can see that we have created an instance of the `Printer` class and then used it to implement the new myFunc method. This is delegation in action and it is simple, but if there are very many methods to delegate, it is also very tedious.

Kotlin will do automatic delegation for you but there are some limitations. The first is that you have to have an interface defined that specifies all of the methods that are going to be delegated. Next you have to have an object that implements the interface. You can get an object that implements the interface either by creating a class that implements the interface and then creating an instance, or by directly creating an object. Once you have the object the derived class can delegate all of the interface methods to the object using the keyword by.

For example, to delegate the Printer methods as before, we would first define an interface that specifies the methods to be automatically delegated:

```
interface Iprinter{
    fun myFunc(mess:String)
}
```

There is just one method in this case, but in general there will be a list of virtual and implemented methods. Next we have to create an object that implements these methods:

```
object printer:Iprinter{
    override fun myFunc(mess: String) {
        println(mess)
    }
}
```

Now we can create a derived class that delegates all of the calls to the methods in the interface to the object that implements the interface:

```
class MyClassA:Iprinter by printer{
    }
```

You can now create an instance of MyClassA and call the myFunc method which is implemented automatically by the system as a call to:

```
printer.myFunc(mess)
```

As already stated, you could create a Printer class that implemented the Iprinter interface and then use an instance as the object that is delegated to. Also notice that while the body of the derived class is empty in this example, you can override the delegated methods and provide a new implementation.

At first sight automatic delegation seems like a powerful feature, but the need to define an interface and then implement it makes it less so. Manual delegation can take any object and use it to create a derived class by delegation even if the base class is final and cannot be used by inheritance. However, automatic delegation needs the base class to implement the interface of methods to be delegated. What this means is that the base class has to be prepared for delegation just as much as for inheritance.

In inheritance a class inherits from another class. but in delegation a class inherits from an object.

Visibility Modifiers, Packages & Modules

In the introduction to this chapter it was explained that the way to tame inheritance is to control access to the inner workings of a class. If the outside world can only make use of what the class does, and not how it does it, then changes to the base class that doesn't alter what it does should be safe.

To control access to classes and class members, Kotlin has four visibility modifiers and while their meanings depend on context their intent is clear:

- `public` – visible everywhere
- `private` – only visible inside the containing unit
- `protected` – same as private but also visible to sub classes
- `internal` – visible to any other code in the same module.

When applied to the members of a class or interface, these have obvious meanings - `public` means that the method or property is accessible and `private` means they aren't. Notice that the inner workings of a method aren't accessible outside of a class even if declared public. This is a special case of the more general rule that local variables are always inaccessible. Also notice that an outer class doesn't see the private members of an inner class.

You can also apply visibility modifiers to constructors.

Kotlin also uses the idea of a package and a module to control access. Packages work roughly the same way that they do in Java. A source file can declare itself a member of a package using:

```
package mypackage.myname
```

Following this the fully qualified name of any class or function has `mypackage.myname` prefixed e.g. `mypackage.myname.MyClass`.

In other languages a package would be called a namespace.

If another source file wants to use something from another package it has to import it:

```
import mypackage.myname.MyClass
```

and to import everything in the package you can use a wildcard:

```
import mypackage.myname.*
```

A class can also be assigned an alias to resolve name clashes:

```
import mypackage.myname.MyClass as AnotherClass
```

Any private properties or functions declared at the top level of a package, i.e. not within a class, are visible throughout the package, but not outside of the package.

Kotlin has one other level of organization – the module. This is more like a compiler unit rather than something abstract. A module can be:

- an IntelliJ IDEA module
- a Maven project
- a Gradle source set
- a set of files compiled with one invocation of the Ant task .

Anything marked as internal in a package is visible everywhere within the module. This is most probably best avoided if possible.

Also notice that Kotlin does not follow the Java practice of storing one class per file and insisting that the file has the same name as the class. This change is a very welcome, but if you are mixing Kotlin and Java you might well have to use the Java convention.

Summary

- Kotlin classes cannot be used as base classes, i.e. cannot be inherited from unless you add the open modifier to the class declaration.

- A class can inherit from one base class only.

- When a class inherits from another, it must arrange to call the base class's primary constructor either directly or via a secondary constructor or via its own primary constructor.

- A class can implement as many interfaces as it needs to.

- A Kotlin interface can include abstract and implemented methods and properties. Any implemented members cannot include state information as there are no backing fields for properties. Any abstract methods or properties have to be implemented.

- If a class inherits a member of the same name from more than one interface then it has to implement it afresh to resolve the clash.

- You can override inherited methods but that method has to be marked open in the base class and override in the derived class.

- As well as interfaces, you can define abstract classes that contain unimplemented abstract methods and properties. The derived class has to implement all of the abstract members.

- Delegation is an alternative to inheritance and Kotlin provides an automatic delegation facility where an object that implements an interface can handle all of the calls to the interface methods on behalf of a class.

- There are a range of visibility modifiers which can be used to restrict access to class members from outside of the class.

Kotlin is a strongly-typed language, but what exactly does this mean. What is "type" and where does it come from? The idea of a type system is something that you can't avoid if you are using classes and objects, and it is worth understanding.

Primitive Data Types

Where do data types come from?

When you first start programming, one of the ideas that seems most difficult is that some primitive data types are somehow incompatible. For example, you can't add a "2" to a 2. The reason is, of course, that the former is a `String` and the latter an `Int`, but to the innocent user they both look like the number two.

This is where the idea of data type originates, but it is not where it ends up.

Primitive data type originates in the different ways that data can be represented. You can represent the idea of "two" either as a string "2", as an integer 2, or as a float 2.0 and so on. The actual bit patterns used to represent the different incarnations of two are different and the operations you can subject them to vary in difficulty of implementation. You could implement an addition operator for numbers represented as strings, but it is much easier to implement addition using ints.

Type in this sense is something of a nuisance, rather than a help, and managing it is a matter of learning how to use functions to perform conversion between the different types so that you can perform operations between them that make sense.

This can be thought of as "active" type conversion because it involves a change of representation.

Such active type conversions are generally implemented as conversion functions. For example, the `toInt` method will convert a suitable string to an integer.

```
val myString="1234"
val myNumber=myString.toInt()
```

Of course, this only works if the string can be parsed as a valid integer. If not the result is an exception. This sort of type conversion is risky but we usually cannot avoid it.

Kotlin strings have a range of type conversion functions and so do the other primitive types.

Notice that you cannot use a Java/C++ style cast to convert types in Kotlin. That is:

```
val myNumber:Int=(Int)myString
```

doesn't mean anything in Kotlin.

The Class Type Hierarchy

When you move beyond primitive types things become more interesting.

Each class that you create can be used to create multiple instances. This is exactly the same as creating multiple instances of an `Int` or a `String`, and these are regarded as different data types. It seems natural to extend the idea so that each class you define is a new data type. In this case, however, the term doesn't really relate to how the data is represented or stored. It has more to do with what instances of the class can do, i.e. what properties and methods they have.

As a class that inherits from another class may be the base class for another class we slowly build up a class hierarchy. All classes start off by inheriting the default `Any` class, more of which later. The result is that classes form a family tree that starts off from `Any` and branches out as each new class inherits from the previous classes.

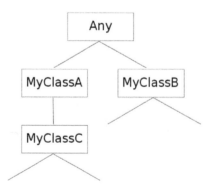

As a class that inherits from another class generally adds properties and methods, you can think of the new derived class as being in some sense "bigger" than the base class. When you define a new class it always has a relationship to the classes it inherits from. At its simplest this could be just

Any, which is the root of the inheritance hierarchy. In many cases, a class will also have a relationship with classes that have been derived from it.

For example:

```
open class MyClassA{
    fun myFunctionA(){}
}
class MyClassB:MyClassA() {
fun myFunctionB(){}
}
```

then MyClassB has all of the methods and properties of MyClassA plus some of its own.

Thus MyClassB is "bigger" than MyClassA because it contains, at least, all of MyClassA.

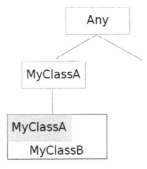

What this means is that you can treat a MyClassB object as if it was in fact a MyClassA object. In this case you would be ignoring the new members added by defining MyClassB by simply restricting your access to MyClassA methods and properties. This "downsizing" of MyClassB is generally called an upcast because it moves you up the object hierarchy towards the root object.

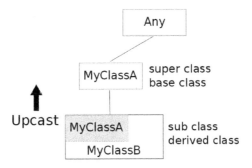

Safe Casting

Casting is the general practice of treating one object as if it was an object of another type. In fact casting is slightly more subtle than this as it involves an object of a given type and a variable that references the object which can be of a different declared type.

If you find you are having problems understanding casting then make sure that you keep in mind the following:

There are always two possible types to consider. The type of the variable used to reference an object and the type of the object being referenced. These need not be the same.

For example consider:

```
var myObjectA:MyClassA
```

this declares the variable myObjectA to be of type MyClassA but at the moment it doesn't reference anything.

If we keep things very simple it could only reference an object of type MyClassA, but this would be very restrictive. As an object of MyClassB has all of the methods and properties of MyClassA objects, we can allow the variable myObjectA to reference an object of MyClassB.

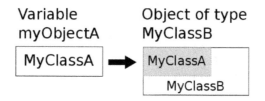

The variable myObjectA can reference an object of type MyClassB by referencing the instance of MyClassA within.

In other words, a derived class can always be used in place of a base class.

Put another way, upcasting is a safe operation. Kotlin allows you to cast an object to a new type using the as operator.

So as long as myObjectB has been created:

```
val myObjectB=myClassB()
```

Then, for example, we can say:

```
myObjectA = myObjectB as MyClassA
```

Now myObjectA actually references an object of type MyClassB, but this doesn't matter as all of the methods that you can use are present in myObjectB. This cast is safe, but only because MyClassB is a derived class of MyClassA. If this wasn't the case then there would be an exception. So this sort of cast isn't safe. You can make it safe using the safe cast operator which casts to a nullable type:

```
var myObjectA:MyClassA?
myObjectA = myObjectB as? MyClassA
```

Now if myObjectB turns out not to be derived from MyClassA, myObjectA is set to null. Notice that you have to declare myObjectA as a nullable type, i.e. as MyClass?, and from this point on you have to play by the rules of nullable types.

Downcasting

If there is upcasting, when you treat a derived class is it it was the base class, there is also downcasting, which is where you use a variable of a base class type to reference a derived type and then cast to that derived type.

The first question that usually comes to mind is, why would you want to do this?

The answer is that you use this technique when you need to apply an algorithm to types of the base class and all derived classes.

For example, if you need to sort some objects into order, you could use a variable of type Any to reference any object.

For example:

```
var myVariable:Any
myVariable=anyObject
```

myVariable can be used to reference any type as all types are sub-types of Any. This is an up cast even if it is the most extreme up cast possible. The down cast comes into the picture when, after doing whatever you want to with the objects of any type, you can down cast to make use of one of their properties.

For example:

```
val myObjectB=MyClassB()
val myObject:Any=myObjectB
(myObject as MyClassB).myFunctionB()
```

here we create an instance of MyClassB and then set myObject to reference it. As myObject is of type Any you can't use it to call any of the methods of MyClassB. However, if we down cast it to the MyClassB type we can now call its methods.

Of course, if myObject isn't referencing an instance of MyClassB, this will fail with an exception. You can use the safe cast to get a null, however.

Downcasting, and using Any references, is a way of implementing generics when you don't have generics. An array of Any will hold references to any type of object and so you can use this to implement "generic" collections.

In languages that do have generics, such as Kotlin, you really should be able to avoid using a down cast. Another use of downcasting is when you pass a base type parameter to a function and then down cast to the particular derived type that has been supplied.

Smart Casts

To make a safe cast you need to know the type of the object you are working with. This turns out to be very easy.

You can use is or !is to test an object's type.

For example, assuming that the variable myObject is of type Any, but references an object of type ClassA:

```
if(myObject is ClassA) {
    (myObject as ClassA).myFunctionA()
}
```

Notice that is tests the type of the object referenced and not the type of the variable referencing it.

You can use this to make both up and downcasting safe, but isn't there something a bit redundant in using an if to test that an object is ClassA and then explicitly casting it to that type?

Smart casts are a Kotlin idiom that save you the time and trouble of an explicit cast. You don't need to do anything extra as the compiler tracks your use of is and !is within conditionals and automatically applies a cast.

Thus the previous example can be written more simply:

```
var myObject:Any=myObjectA
if(myObject is MyClassA) {
        myObject.myFunctionA()
}
```

It can even apply an automatic cast within a conditional expression:

```
myObject is MyclassA && myObject.myFunctionA()==0
```

You can use smart casts within if statements, when and while. The compiler also checks to make sure that the variable that is the subject of the is cannot change before it is used.

You don't have to make use of smart casts.

You can always include an as or as? where a smart cast would apply.

Should you use smart casts?

Smart casts do reduce the amount of typing, but it could be argued that they result in code that is less clear. I would advise always making casts explicit.

Overriding & Casting – Virtual methods

Inheritance in Kotlin is always "virtual" in the sense used in C++ and C#. That is, the method called depends on the type of the object and not the type of the variable at compile time.

For example, if we have two classes:

```kotlin
open class MyClassA{
    open fun myFunctionA(){println("A")}
}
class MyClassB:MyClassA() {
    override fun myFunctionA(){println("B")}
    fun myFunctionB(){println("B")}
}
```

The derived MyClassB overrides the inherited myFunctionA.

Now consider:

```kotlin
val myObjectB=MyClassB()
var myObject:MyClassA
myObject=myObjectB
```

In this case we have a variable of type MyClassA referencing an object of type MyClassB i.e. a down cast.

What do you think happens when we call the overridden function?

```kotlin
myObject.myFunctionA()
```

If you are a C++ or C# programmer then you will expect that it is the original MyClassA version of the overridden function which is used. That is, you see an "A" printed.

If you are a Java or a Kotlin programmer, you can't really understand why the answer should be anything other than the new overridden version of the function as defined in MyClassB, i.e. you expect to see a "B" printed and are mystified as to why "A" would ever be considered a correct result.

The reason for this strange behavior is that, in C++ and C#, methods are bound to variables at compile time and, as myObject is of type MyClassA, it calls the functions of MyClassA and not those of MyClassB. To produce the behavior we get in Kotlin in C++ and C#, you have to declare the method "virtual" which is another meaning of this popular term. This causes the compiler to bind the variable to the methods of the object it is referencing at run time. Not as efficient but much more logical.

In Kotlin the methods used depend on the object that the variable references at run time, not its compile-time type.

Another, potentially confusing, way to say this is that all Kotlin methods are "virtual" in the sense of C++ and C#.

Function Types

One big difference between Kotlin and other more traditional object-oriented languages is that it allows you to treat functions as types. This is necessary when you allow for functions which are not methods such as lambdas.

If you can pass a function as a parameter you need to specify its type.

The type of a function is just its signature plus its return type.

For example:

```
(Int,String)->Unit
```

is a function type that accepts an `Int` and a `String` and returns `Unit`.

You can use function types to define variables and parameters which can be used to reference a function of that type.

For example:

```
val add:(Int,Int)->Int
add = {a:Int,b:Int->a+b}
println(add(1,2))
```

This declares a variable called `add` which can be a reference to a function that takes two ints and returns an `Int`. The next line defines just such a function and the final line makes use of it.

Function types can be difficult to read and it is usually a good idea to use a type alias to make their meaning more obvious.

Type Aliases

One of the big problems in programming is naming. You need to use descriptive names. but usually this mean very long names. How often you find class names like:

```
class NewCustomerInTheNorthernSector{
```

You could use a `typealias` to add a shortened form of the name:

```
typealias NCusNorth=NewCustomerInTheNorthernSector
```

You could, but it probably isn't a good idea. Short names are usually bad and having two names for something is usually even worse.

Notice that a `typealias` cannot be local or nested within another structure.

There is some justification for using `typealias` in connection with generics, as their names tend to become very long due to the need to repeat type parameters.

Another good use for `typealias` is to give a meaningful name to a function type.

For example, in the previous section we had a function which accepted two ints and return an `Int`. We can make this more descriptive by defining:

```
typealias arithmetic=(Int,Int)->Int
```

Now we can define the add function as:

```
val add: arithmetic
add = {a:Int,b:Int->a+b}
println(add(1,2))
```

which gives you a much clearer idea of what the function is for, even if as succeeds in hiding the signature.

Summary

- The idea of type arises from the different ways that apparently the same data can be represented e.g. "2" and 2.

- This idea has been extended into a complex system of hierarchical types based on class and inheritance.

- A derived class can (nearly) always be used in place of a base class.

- A variable of one type can be used to reference a class of a different but related type.

- Changing type from a derived type to a base type is called upcasting and is generally a safe operation.

- Changing type from a base class to a derived type is called downcasting and is only safe if the base class is of the type you are casting to.

- Kotlin provides smart casting which will cast to the type you have just tested for.

- You can test an object type using `is` or `!is`.

- You can explicitly cast to another type using `as` or the safe type operator `as?`

- All methods in Kotlin are what would be called "virtual" in some other languages. This means that the method called depends on the run-time type of the object referenced, and not the compile-time type of the variable doing the referencing.

- You can define function types as `(parameter types) ->return type`

- A `typealias` assigns a name to a type.

Generics are an essential part of any modern language. Kotlin has generics and at first they look like any other languages generics but as with most Kotlin features they have some interesting differences.

Why Generics?

We start out programming not really worrying too much about type and then it becomes central to everything we do. Everything has a type and when you write code it works with a specific set of types.

However, some algorithms are the same no matter what type they work with.

For example, a sorting algorithm doesn't really care what it is sorting as long as it has a way to decide if one element is bigger than another. Yet in a strongly-typed language you have to write a sort routine for each type you want to sort.

Of course, this isn't what happens. If you want to do something in a type-independent way then you can give up strong typing and work with Any and downcasting.

Unfortunately an array of Any objects isn't very useful as Any has a very restricted set of methods and these are all you can use. To make a typed approach to creating generics work, you have to have a base class that has the methods you want to use to manipulate all of its derived classes, and class hierarchies generally aren't designed with this in mind.

For example, Number is the top level class for any numeric type in Kotlin, but it doesn't have a comparison operator. This means you can' t write a sorting function using it.

As Number has an equality operator, you can, however, write a find function:

```
fun find(a:Array<out Number>,Target:Number):Int{
    for( i in a.indices){
        if( a[i]==Target ){
            return i
        }
    }
    return -1
}
```

This works because the array type is `Array<out Number>` and `Number` is the base class for all numerics. Don't worry about the use of `out` in the array declaration, it is explained later.

The problem is that, as a Kotlin array is defined as a generic, we can't actually avoid generics in this implementation.

With this function definition we can now call `find` using an array of elements of any numeric type.

For example:

```
var b = arrayOf(1, 2, 3)
println(find(b, 2))
```

or:

```
var b = arrayOf(1.1, 2.1, 3.2)
println(find(b, 2.1))
```

However, if you try:

```
var b = arrayOf('A','B','C')
println(find(b, 'A'))
```

you will find that it doesn't work for `Array<Char>`.

To make it work you would have to change `Number` to `Any`, as `Char` isn't a numeric even if it has a comparison operator.

This is a completely general approach to implementing algorithms that work with a range of objects types. All you have to do is write a function that accepts the base class for all of the objects and work with it. If you want to access any of the methods beyond the base class you will need a downcast. This approach is workable but not particularly flexible.

Generics is a purpose-built solution for writing general algorithms that work on a range of types in a type-safe way. However, it is worth pointing out that generics doesn't offer much more than working with variables that reference `Any` and often imposes restrictions which have to be overcome to implement what you want. It is not the perfect solution to type-free programming.

Basic Generics

The basic idea of generics is very simple – it allows type parameters in class, interface and function definitions. To make use of such generic declarations you have to supply real types for the type parameters at the time they are used.

A type parameter is defined by being enclosed in **< >** used as brackets and can be used anywhere a type specification can be used.

So for example the function that we used earlier to find an element in an array can be re-written:

```
fun <T> find(a: Array<T>, Target: T): Int {
      for (i in a.indices) {
          if (a[i] == Target) return i
      }
      return -1
   }
```

The <T> at the start declares the type parameter. You don't have to use T and you can have as many type parameters as you like. Within the function definition, the type parameter is just used as T without angle brackets. Notice that Array is now clearly a generic type as it too has a type parameter that we have to specify using the same angle bracket form.

Following this we can call the generic function:

```
println(find<Int>(b, 2))
```

which will work assuming that b is an array of ints.

Class and interface generic declarations work in the same way – add a type parameter in angle brackets at the start of the declaration and use the parameter as if was a type in the body of the declaration.

For example:

```
class MyClassA<T>{
    fun myMethod(a:T){
    }
}
```

declares a class with a single type parameter and a method that accepts a single parameter of that type. You can include a base class and interfaces within the class definition.

That is, apart from the use of the type parameter, the class declaration is standard. The same is true for a generic interface.

Now we come to the big restriction inherent in using a generic. As the type parameter is unknown at the time of declaring the class, interface or function, you can't use any of its methods other then the ones supported by Any.

So, for example, if you try to write:

```
fun <T> add(a:T,b:T):T{
        return a+b
}
```

the result is an error message saying the system can't work out what a+b is.

That is, when you are writing a generic, <T> is the same as Any. This isn't unreasonable as, without knowing what T is, how can the system determine at compile time how to implement the + operator?

A second problem is that at run time the type of any parameter passed to the function is lost. That is, if you pass an Int as a and b, you can't discover this at run time – the types of the parameters are erased. This obviously enough, is called type erasure and it is how Java implements generics.

Generic Properties

As a consequence of not being able to do anything to a type that you don't know, also notice that you cannot define a standard generic property within a class. The reason is that it would have to be initialized, and what do you initialize an unknown type to?

That is:

```
class MyClass<T>{
 var myProp:T
}
```

will cause the compiler to insist that you initialize the property or declare it virtual and you cannot create an instance of T as you don't at this stage know what T is. If you set myProp to a nullable type then you can set it to Any:

```
var myProp:T?=Any()
```

but this forces all instances to have a property of type Any, which isn't really what you want.

What you can do is create a property using the primary constructor, as this forces an initialization when the constructor is called, and Kotlin is satisfied that the property is initialized:

```
class MyClass<T>(val myProp: T) {}
```

After this you can create an instance with a property of the correct type:

```
var a=MyClass<Int>(12)
println(a.myProp)
println(a.javaClass)
```

prints 12 and "Int".

So, if you want a generic property, use the primary constructor.

Supplying Generic Actions

So how can generics implement anything useful if you cannot apply any type specific actions to generic entities?

One very general answer is to use specific implementations of a generic function type that performs the operation you require on specific types.

For example, you can't use a+b when the types are unknown but you can rewrite a custom add function as:

```
fun <T> add(a:T,b:T,op:(T,T)->T):T{
        return op(a,b)
    }
```

Notice now that the third parameter is a function that takes two parameters of type T and returns a T. This is a generic formulation of a function that takes two parameters of the same type and applies a function to them that that is also passed as a parameter. The function that is passed in its turn takes two parameters of the specified typo and returns a result of the same type. All of this is fine as no knowledge of the type T is used in this – it works for any type, including Any.

Now lets try adding two ints:
```
add<Int>(1,2,sumInt)
```

The first two parameters are fine as they are ints but the third isn't defined and it needs to be a function that accepts two ints and returns an Int.

This is easy to define:
```
var  sumInt: (Int,Int)->Int  = {a,b-> a+b}
```

This is a lambda, see Chapter 11. The lambda is defined within the curly brackets and it is a function of the correct type i.e. (T,T)->T where T is Int.

Now everything works, and:
```
add<Int>(1,2,sumInt)
```

returns 3.

Notice that the function you pass is not a generic – it has a definite type, even at compile time. The downside is that you need to define an auxiliary function for each of the types that you actually want to process. You can make this look more like a fully generic solution by defining a typealias:

```
typealias arithmetic<T> =(T,T)->T
var sumInt:arithmetic<Int> = {a,b-> a+b}

fun <T> add(a:T,b:T,op:arithmetic<T>):T{
        return op(a,b)
    }
```

Once again the sumInt is fully defined at compile time including the type of its parameters.

Generic Constraints

The problem is that when we use a type parameter like T it can be any type. This is the advantage of generics but it means that, if we want to use any operations on a particular type we have to implement specific functions that work with the type.

The reason we can't call any methods on a generic type is that the compiler has no idea what the type is at run time. We can relax this by applying generic constraints to the type parameter which limits what sort of types are allowable. Knowing that the type parameter must be a particular type or a subtype of that type we can allow methods to be used secure in the knowledge that the methods will exist at run time.

The only constraints that Kotlin provides are generally called "upper bounds". You can follow the type parameter with a type specifier. This gives the base class for the set of types that the type parameter can be.

In other words the type parameter has to be either the specified base class or a class derived from it. This allows the compiler to infer that an object described by the type parameter can have any of the methods of the base class and so these can be used in the generic.

For example:

```
fun <T:MyClassA> myFunction(a:T):T{...
```

defines a function that accepts an object of type MyClassA as a parameter or anything derived from it. Notice that this is the same as:

```
fun myFunction(a:MyClassA){..
```

since a derived class can be used in place of a base class.

Also notice that constraints have the same problem as using a base class as a type. If the base class doesn't implement the methods you want to use then you can't make use of them.

For example, you still can't implement a generic add function because Number doesn't define an addition function. That is

```
fun <T:Number> add(x:T,y:T):T{
  return x+y
}
```

doesn't work because Number doesn't define an addition operation. Even with constraints you are still at the mercy of the way the class hierarchy is constructed in what you can easily implement as a generic.

As well as a single base class constraint you can also specify multiple constraints using `where`.

For example:

```
fun <T> myMax(a:T,b:T):T
    where  T:Number,
           T:Comparable<T>{
        return if(a>b) a else b
    }
```

In this case T has to be derived from the `Number` class and also implement the `Comparable` interface. All of the usual number classes satisfy this constraint. With the constraint in place we can use the greater than operator to return the maximum.

Also notice that `Comparable` is itself a generic interface and this form of constraint would be difficult to implement in any other way.

This is more powerful but notice that we still can't implement a generic sum function because there isn't a Summable interface. Each of the numeric types implements its own plus function. It would seem reasonable that any `Number` type would have a plus function, but it isn't defined in `Number` or in a `Summable` interface.

This is a completely general problem. If you want to write a generic that works with all of the derived classes of an upper bound then the class that forms the upper bound has to have all of the methods you want to use.

Covariance & Contravariance

This is one of the most complicated of the generic topics and it is made more complicated by the use of some advanced sounding terminology. However, it isn't as difficult as many explanations and examples would have you believe. Even so, many users, and even designers of generic classes, don't have to understand what is going on at first. so come back and read this when you need to and once you have a good grasp of inheritance.

The first thing to understand is that inputs behave differently to outputs.

If you recall, derived classes are "bigger" than base classes because they have everything that the base class has, and possibly some additional methods and properties. You can think of this as defining a partial order on the classes.

If class B is derived from class A you can write A>B, indicating that A is higher in the class hierarchy than B, even though B potentially has actually more methods than A. This is confusing, but it is widely used. If A>B then B can be used anywhere that A can - this is the Liskov Substitution principle, and it is more of an ideal than a principle or a practical reality.

You can extend this idea and say that any entity B that can be used anywhere A can, satisfies A>B even if A isn't in any other sense a base entity for B. Now consider the following function:

```
fun MyFunction1(a:MyClassA){
  …
  create myObjectB an instance of MyClassB
  return myObjectB
}
```

As `MyClassB` is derived from `MyClassA`, i.e. `MyClassA>MyClassB`, we can pass in an instance of `MyClassB` because it has everything an instance of `MyClassA` has and more.

It is fine for the function to treat the `MyClassB` instance as a `MyClassA` instance. The output returned by the function is an instance of `MyClassB` and, by the same reasoning, the calling program is safe to treat this as a `MyClassA`.

Looking at this in a slightly different way, what does it mean for the function?

Consider the function redefined to accept a `MyClassB` instance with no other changes. That is:

```
MyFunction2(a:MyClassB){ … }
```

Now you can see that, as `MyFunction1` can accept an instance of `MyClassB`, it can trivially be used anywhere `MyFunction2` is, but `MyFunction2` cannot accept a `MyClassA` and cannot be used anywhere a `MyFunction1` is.

This means that we can regard:

```
MyFunction2>MyFunction1
```

Notice that:

```
MyClassA>MyClassB
```

has resulted in the conclusion that:

```
MyFunction1(MyClassA)< MyFunction2(MyClassB)
```

This is called contravariance and in general we say that if A>B means that G(A)<G(B) where G is a type that involves the other classes, then the relationship is contravariant.

Put in even simpler language, if you construct a new type involving an existing type then it is contravariant if the construction reverses the "use in place of" relationship. Inputs are generally contravariant for the reasons outlined above.

Now consider the same argument but for the output parameter.

For `MyFunction1` this is of type `MyClassB`. A function, `MyFunction2`, that returns a `MyClassA` but is otherwise identical, cannot be used in its place, but `MyFunction1` can be used in place of `MyFunction2`. This means that `MyFunction2>MyFunction1` because `MyFunction1` can be used anywhere `MyFunction2` can.

In this case we have:

`MyClassA>MyClassB`

which implies:

`MyFunction2(){return MyClassA}>MyFunction1(){return MyClassB}`

This is an example of covariance and in simple terms this means if you construct a new type involving an existing type, then it is covariant if the construction follows the same the "use in place of" relationship.

In general, outputs are covariant.

Now that you have looked at the way that a change to a function affects its type, we can generalize the idea of covariance and contravariance to any situation, not just where functions are involved.

Suppose we have two types A and B and we have a modification, or transformation G, that we can make to both of them to give new types G(A) and G(B).

- ♦ If G is a covariant transformation we have A>B implies G(A)>G(B). Outputs are covariant.

- ♦ If G is a contravariant transformation then we have A>B implies G(A)<G(B). Inputs are contravariant.

- ♦ It is also possible that neither relationship applies. That is A>B doesn't imply anything about the relationship between G(A) and G(B). In this case G is referred to as invariant – which isn't really a good name.

In the case of our example we had two transformations G1, which converted the type into the input parameter – a contravariant transform, and G2, which converted the type into the return result – a covariant transform.

It can be very difficult to keep all of this in your head when reasoning about particular data types – arrays for example – but eventually you get used to it.

Covariant & Contravariant Generics

What else is a generic declaration than a transformation from a type T to another type G(T)?

For example `Array<T>` converts an `Int` into `Array<Int>`.

Next we come to the question of whether an array, considered as a transformation on the type of its element, is covariant, contravariant or invariant.

After all, it has to be one of these three, even if you don't know what covariant, contravariant or invariant actually mean!

Put in its most practical terms, given that `Int` is a derived class of `Any`:

```
Array<Int>
```

could be a derived class of:

```
Array<Object>
```

which would make `Array` covariant.

It could be a super class of:

```
Array<Object>
```

which would make `Array` contravariant

or it could have no relationship with:

```
Array<Object>
```

which would make `Array` invariant

As already said, you have to answer this question, even if you don't use the academic sounding terms taken from category theory and physics.

In Java and most other languages `Array<Int>` can be treated as if it was `Array<Any>` and this means it is covariant. This works well when array use fits in with the idea that outputs are covariant.

For example, consider this code, which would be perfectly acceptable if arrays were treated as covariant:

```
var a:Array<Any>
var b:Array<Int>
b= arrayOf(1,2,3)
a=b
```

Note: this doesn't actually work as written because in Kotlin arrays are invariant not covariant, but it illustrates the point.

This assignment is safe as long as you only use the variable `a` to access the array and not store anything new in it. That is, `a[i]` is treated as `Any` and you can use any of the methods that `Any` has, and the underlying Int certainly has these.

However, if you assign to an element of `a` then things are potentially more risky. You can assign any object you like as all objects are derived from `Any`. This leaves our `Int` array in something of a potential mess.

Consider what happens if we assign a `String` to an element and then try and access it as if it was an `Int`. The result would be a run time exception and there is no way that this could be picked up at compile time.

This is clearly not a good idea.

You can also come to the conclusion that treating the array as contravariant isn't a good idea either. In this case the problem arises when you try and access an element of the array and treat it like a derived class of `Int` only to discover that it is just an `Int`.

This is the reason why Kotlin defines an array as invariant and this makes the above code illegal as is any code that assigns an `Array<T>` variable to anything other than another `Array<T>`.

Controlling Variance – in & out

All generics in Kotlin are, by default, invariant. That is, they are their own type and not related to anything else in the hierarchy.

This is safe in that you can pick up type errors at compile time and you can't generate a run-time error by using the wrong type. However, it stops you doing things that are type safe. It all depends on whether the type parameter in question is used as an input, an output or both.

The idea is that if a type is used only as an input then it is safe to treat the generic as contravariant. If it is only used as an output then it can be used covariantly and if it is both you have no choice but to treat the generic as invariant.

Kotlin provides two modifiers, `in` and `out`, which allow you to mark type parameters as contravariant or covariant.

Note: You can only use type variance modifiers on generic classes and interfaces, not in generic functions.

To see how this works we need to create a sample generic class that has a read-only property:

```
class MyClass<T>( myParam: T) {
    private var t:T=myParam
        fun read():T{
            return t
        }
}
```

The reason for the strange implementation of a read-only property is that we want to convert it to a write-only property in a moment, and the usual way of implementing a property doesn't support this.

By default this generic is invariant. What this means is that:

```
var b=MyClass<Int>(1)
var a:MyClass<Any>
a=b
```

is trying to treat `MyClass<Int>` as a derived class of `MyClass<Any>` produces a compile-time error:

```
18
19              var b=MyClass<Int>( myParam: 1)
20              var a:MyClass<Any>
21          💡  a=b
22
23     Type mismatch.
23
24     Required:  MyClass<Any>
24
25     Found:     MyClass<Int>
25
```

Similarly:

```
var b=MyClass<Any>(1)
var a:MyClass<Int>
a=b
```

That is, trying to treat `MyClass<Any>` as a derived class of `MyClass<Int>` also doesn't work in the same way.

As our class has a read-only property, treating it as contravariant seems like a reasonable thing to do and we can by using the `out` modifier.

```
class MyClass<out T>( myParam: T) {
   private var t:T=myParam
       fun read():T{
           return t
       }
}
```

If the `T` type parameter is used anywhere in the class definition in a way that is an input, you will see a warning that you are using out incorrectly.

With the `out` modifier we can now treat the class as covariant and:

```
var b=MyClass<Int>(1)
var a:MyClass<Any>
a=b
println(a.read())
```

works perfectly.

Now if we change T to be an input only and add the in modifier:

```
class MyClass<in T>( myParam: T) {
    private var t:T=myParam
        fun write(t:T){
            this.t=t
        }
}
```

we now have a contravariant generic class. This allows us to write:

```
var b=MyClass<Any>(1)
var a:MyClass<Int>
a=b
a.write(2)
```

That's all there is to the use of in and out – they simply select contravariant or covariant behavior for the generic on that parameter.

This use of in and out when the generic is declared is called declaration-site variance, and it is useful when you are creating generics, but what about when you are just consuming them – use-site variance?

Type Projections

Type projections solve the problem of changing the behavior of a generic class after it has been declared. It also allows you to take a generic entity and while it might not use the type parameter as a pure input or output you can promise to use it as strictly input or output.

For example, consider the array. This is by default invariant and you cannot sensibly redefine its declaration to make it contravariant or covariant because it makes little sense to have array elements that are exclusively read- or write-only. Instead you can use in and out in type modifiers to mark types that will only act as consumers or producers and hence define the type's variance.

For example:

```
var a:Array<Any>
var b = Array<Int>(10,{0})
a=b
```

produces a compile-time error because Array is invariant.

You can't change the fact that arrays are invariant, but you can define the type of a so that it is a consumer:

```
var a:Array<out Any>
var b = Array<Int>(10,{0})
a=b
```

The out modifier says that a will only be used to access array elements and this is safe because the underlying elements are ints which, as a derived type of Any, have all the methods and properties required.

107

What is important here is to realize that this projection is mostly a trick to allow the upcast to pass the compiler's type checking. The elements of the array referenced by a are still ints. What stops you from assigning to a[i] even though you have promised you won't? The simple answer is that a[i] is regarded as an Int so assigning, say, a string to it will fail because the types are incompatible.

You can try the same trick with a covariant in:

```
var a:Array<in Int>
var b = Array<Any>(10,{0})
a=b
```

without the in this too generates a compile-time error. With the in it compiles and you can store values of type Any in elements of a. The compiler allows the assignment but in this case there is nothing to stop you from using a as a source or a consumer of values. That is:

```
a[1]="abcd"
println(a[1])
```

works and if you expect a[1] to be an Int just because a is Array<in Int> you are going to be disappointed. This type projection doesn't work as well as it could.

If you use a projection as a function parameter, then the compiler will also check that you are playing by the rules. For example:

```
fun myFunc(myparam:MyClass<out Any>){
    println(myparam.read())
    myparam.write(10)
}
```

In this case the compiler will complain about the use of write which attempts to change the value.

Similarly if you define the function as:

```
fun myFunc(myparam:MyClass<in Int>){
    println(myparam.read()+1)
    myparam.write(10)
}
```

then the compiler will complain about the + operator as we cannot guarantee that the value is numeric.

The in and out modifiers used as type projections simply allow the up and downcasting of the type and tell you that it is safe to set or get elements.

The * Projection

Finally we have the * projection. This can be used to ask the compiler to treat every instance of the generic as a subtype.

In most situations this cannot be allowed without some additional restrictions as it could result in a run time type error.

The rule is that for an invariant, type MyClass<*> is like MyClass<out Upper> for reading and MyClass<in Nothing> where Upper is the upper bound if there is one and Any otherwise. The use of Nothing signifies a class that cannot be instantiated and represents a value that cannot exist. It is there to allow the compiler to show an error if you try to assign to it.

For a covariant type T, MyClass<*> is equivalent to MyClass<out Upper> and you can read values but not write them.

For a contravariant type I MyClass<*> is equivalent to MyClass<in Nothing> and you cannot read or write anything.

For example:

```
var a:Array<*>
var b = Array<Any>(10,{0})
a=b
a[1]="abcd"
println(a[1])
```

As Array<Any> is a subtype of Array<*>.

Similarly

```
var a:Array<*>
var b = Array<Int>(10,{0})
a=b
```

works because Array<Int> is a subtype of Array<*> but you cannot assign a string to a[i] because this is still regarded as an Int.

The * projection allows you to treat any generic as a subtype, but in a type safe way.

For another example consider:

```
class MyClass<T>( myParam: T) {
    private var t:T=myParam
    fun read():T{
        return t
    }
    fun write(t:T){
        this.t=t
    }
}
```

This is neither covariant nor contravariant as it has both read and write methods but we can still treat an instance of it as a subclass of MyClass<*>:

```
var a: MyClass<*>
var b = MyClass<Int>(1)
a = b
a.write(10)
println(a.read())
a.write("abcd")
```

In this case the up cast a=b is fine as MyClass<Int> is a subclass of MyClass<*> and the call to read works but the call to write fails because write still accepts a as an Int parameter. Again type projection doesn't alter the type or behavior of the underlying object.

At this point you might be wondering what the point is of the * projection? The most common use case is to write a function which can accept all instances of a generic.

For example:

```
fun myFunc(a:MyClass<*>){...
```

can accept any MyClass<T> object, no matter what T is. However, what you can do within the function depends on the variance of MyClass. If it is invariant or covariant you can read T from it, but not write to T. If it is contravariant you can't access T at all.

Notice that when <*> is used in a function the compiler really can't infer anything about the type at all and so it has to enforce the rules in a different way.

Summary

- Generics are an attempt at allowing algorithms that work with a range of types to be written in a type safe way.

- Kotlin generics, like those in Java and most other languages, make use of type parameters indicated by <T>. These are used in generic code as if they were a type specifier and assigned a value when the generic code is used to operate on a particular type.

- The big problem in using generics is that you cannot assume anything about the type T even though you may know at run time what it is. This means you cannot call any methods or use properties beyond that possessed by Any.

- Generic properties pose a particular problem because you cannot even initialize them as you don't know their type at compile time.

- You can create generic properties but only if you include them in the primary constructor so that they are guaranteed to be initialized at run time.

- One approach to creating generic methods or functions that can do more than just work with Any is to pass a generic action function which has a defined type at compile time.

- A second approach is to use type constraints. Kotlin provides the upper bound constraint which specifies the base class that the type must be derived from. This allows you to use the methods and properties of the base class within the generic code.

- Variance is all about how data structures relate to one another when they are composed of related types. That is, if you construct a new type involving an existing type then it is contravariant if the construction reverses the "use in place of" relationship. If you construct a new type involving an existing type then it is covariant if the construction follows the same the "use in place of" relationship. If there is no relationship then the construct is invariant.

- Inputs tend to be contravariant, outputs covariant and general read/write types are invariant.

- Generics and arrays in Kotlin are invariant by default.

- You can modify this default variance by using the in and out modifiers when you declare the type – declaration-site variance.

- You can also modify the variance when you use a type using the same in and out modifiers – use-site variance or projections.

- The * projection lets you pass any instance of a generic, no matter what its type.

Chapter 9

Collections, Iterators, Sequences & Ranges

In the previous chapter we dug deep into generics, but the most common use of generics is to build collection classes, and in this respect Kotlin has everything Java has and some more.

Collection Basics

Generics were invented largely to allow us to implement collections. In this particular case most of the problems of using generic types simply vanish because all we want to do is store a reference to an object and perhaps move it around. In general, the question of calling methods defined on the object involved in the generic only arises as a side issue. In other words, collections store objects without worrying too much about what they actually do.

A collection organizes a set of objects.

The objects are stored as a set of references.

In Java, collections are distinct from simple arrays. In Kotlin, an array is a class like other collection classes, but it is implemented as a primitive Java array when compiled, for reasons of efficiency.

In other words, a Kotlin array behaves a little like a collection, but it has all of the characteristics of a Java array because that is what it is.

However, this said, there are still important differences between a Kotlin array and the collection classes. In particular, an array is static and it cannot change its allocated size. The other collection classes are dynamic and can expand and contract according to what is stored in them. An array also stores primitive types as values, this is why it is efficient. Collection classes, on the other hand, store references to objects. If you do use primitive types in a collection class, then it is boxed by a wrapper class.

Another big difference is that Kotlin provides two versions of the Java collections – a mutable one, which is like the corresponding Java class; and an immutable one, which is new in Kotlin. If you simply use a collection class then you will get the immutable one by default. To use the mutable version you have to change the name to have the word `Mutable` in front of it e.g. `List` is immutable and `MutableList` is mutable.

It is important to understand that the immutable collections that Kotlin provides aren't really immutable in the strongest possible sense. They are simply the standard Java mutable collections with the restriction that they are read-only. Hence here are no efficiency gains to be had from using immutable collections, i.e. no memory optimizations, and there are ways that immutable collections can be modified by casting to a mutable type.

What this means is that in Kotlin, by providing read-only mutable objects, simply provide a level of protection against accidental changes to data.

Immutable collections are also covariant and you can assign a collection of a given type to a collection of its base type.

Finally, it is worth pointing out that while Kotlin collections are based on Java collections, Kotlin adds many methods, using extension methods, see the next chapter, to the collection classes. This extends what you can do without losing compatibility with Java.

List & MutableList

Although the `Collection` class is the base class for all the collection classes, the `List` and `MutableList` are the pair that best serve as an introduction. You can't create an instance of the `Collection` class; it is mostly useful as the base type for any additional collections you might want to create.

The `List` is just like an array but it can change its size. The elements of a `List` have a fixed type, the immutable version is covariant and the mutable version is invariant. As the `List` doesn't have a set function, it cannot change its size and so it really is just like a covariant version of a standard array. Notice that at the moment `List` is implemented not as a Java array but as a Java ArrayList, which isn't as efficient because it is still a dynamic data structure.

The first problem with using any of the collections is how to create an instance. This follows the pattern introduced with the array class. That is, each collection class has its `collectionOf` function which converts a comma separated list of values into an object of the collection's type.

For example:

```
var a=listOf("x","y","z")
```

creates a `List<String>` with three elements.

The second way is to use the constructor and supply a function which can be used to initialize the collection. That is:

```
List(size, init)
```

creates a list of the specified *size* and uses the *init* function to initialize each element in turn.

For example:

```
var a=List(10,{""})
```

creates a List<String> with 10 elements all set to the null string. The {""} is a lambda function that returns the null string.

You can, of course, use a more complicated initialization function.

For example:

```
var b = List<String>(10,{i->(i.toString())})
```

creates a list of 10 elements initialized to "0" to "9".

As List is read-only, it is covariant which means you can cast it to a List of a super type. For example:

```
var b = List<String>(10,{i->(i.toString())})
var c:List<Any>
c=b
```

Notice that the system still "knows" that c is of type List<String> at run time.

List behaves like an array and it is only when we start to use MutableList that we get any really new behavior.

You can create a MutableList in the same way as a List:

```
var a:MutableList<String> = mutableListOf("x","y","z")
var b = MutableList<String>(10,{i->(i.toString())})
```

The big difference is that you can make the MutableList bigger.

If you are familiar with more permissive languages such as JavaScript you might think that this allows you to reference elements that don't exist. You can't. To add an element beyond what are already there you have to use the add method:

```
var a:MutableList<String> = mutableListOf("x","y","z")
a.add("k")
```

which produces ["x","y","z","k"].

The add method adds to the end of the collection by default, but you can insert an element at a specific position.

For example:

```
var a:MutableList<String> = mutableListOf("x","y","z")
a.add(1,"k")
```

produces ["x","k","y","z"]

You can also use the addAll method to add a list of elements in one go. To shrink the collection you can use remove and clear which remove one instance of an element and all of the elements respectively.

The sublist(start,end) method gives you the ability to extract a sub-list.

Unlike other languages there is no support for "slicing notation".

It is important that you don't try to make use of an element that doesn't exist. If you do, the result is a run-time exception. You can check the size of a collection using the `size` property and the `lastindex` property.

As well as these basic methods and properties there are a number of extensions that take us well beyond what is available in Java. Notable are the sorting methods, the binary search method, and a set of methods that let you find and count elements. They are all worth knowing about and very straightforward in their use.

As already mentioned `List` isn't completely immutable.

For example, if you explicitly cast to `MutableList` then you can change elements:

```
var a=listOf("x","y","z")
var b:MutableList<String>
b=a as MutableList<String>
b[1]="k"
println(a)
```

This results in `[x,k,z]` being printed and immutable `List` a has been changed.

If you want a `List` to be immutable make sure it isn't cast to `MutableList`.

The Collections

The `List` a good archetypal collection class, but what else do we have?

As in Java there are three types of collection:

- `List`
- `Map`
- `Set`

The `List` has already been described, and it is an ordered list of elements much like an array.

A `Map` is a set of key value pairs, sometimes called a dictionary, hash map or associative array in other languages.

A `Set` is an unordered list which allows you to store values in it as if it was a simple container. The key feature of a `Set` is that it doesn't allow duplicates.

Let's take a brief look at maps and sets.

Map

```
Map<K, out V>
MutableMap<K, V>
```

Map is one of the most useful collection objects and most sophisticated. You can store a set of key/value pairs and retrieve and store values using the key. Key values have to be unique, and you can only store one value per key. The key is covariant in Map and both types are invariant in MutableMap.

Creating an instance of Map works in the same general way, but there are no constructors. Instead you have to use the mapOf and mutableMapOf builder functions, which create objects that implement the Map or MutableMap interfaces.

For example:

```
var a=mapOf("a" to 1,"b" to 2)
```

The to operator is a function that converts the left and right objects into a key/value Pair. You can create your own Pair objects and use them in mapOf if you want to:

```
var e=Pair("c",3)
var a=mapOf("a" to 1,"b" to 2, e)
```

To access an element you can use the get(K) and put(K,V) methods. You can also set up a map using:

```
var b= mutableMapOf<String,Int>()
b.put("a",1)
```

and so on.

Set

```
Set<out E>
MutableSet<E>
```

Set is an unordered collection that doesn't allow duplicates.

As in the case of Map you cannot call a constructor to create a Set. Instead, there are builder functions setOf and mutableSetOf.

For example:

```
var a=setOf<String>("a","b","c")
```

You can use add(E) and remove(E) to add and remove elements.

The only real reason for building and using a set is to keep track of which elements are in it. To do this you generally use the contains(E) method which is common to all collections.

An alternative way of creating a set is:

```
var a= mutableSetOf<String>()
a.add("a")
```

If you try and add the same element more than once then you don't generate an exception, but there is still only one instance stored in the set.

In addition to Kotlin supported collection types `List`, `Map` and `Set`, there are also type aliases for the Java types ArrayList, HashMap, HashSet, LinkedHashMap, LinkedHashSet and RandomAccess. These are essentially different implementations of the same collection types and work in the same way. Also notice that currently the Kotlin `List` is implemented as a Java ArrayList.

Iterators

Collections of objects usually have an iterator to allow you to step through each object in turn. In fact, you can have an iterator that isn't associated with a collection of objects and simply generates the next object on demand.

An iterator has to have at least two functions – next which returns the next object, and `hasNext` which returns `true` if there is a next object.

For example the Kotlin `for` can be written as:

```
while(it.hasNext()){
 e=it.Next()
 instructions that use e
}
```

For example:

```
var a= mutableListOf<String>("a","b","c")
for(e in a.iterator()) println(e)

var it=a.iterator()
while(it.hasNext()){
    var e=it.next()
    println(e)
 }
```

The two loops work in the same way. The iterator method returns an initialized iterator for the collection. You can use this to retrieve each element in turn. Notice that you can't reset an iterator to the first value – you simply create a new instance. If this behavior doesn't suit you then simply include a `start` and/or `end` parameter in the constructor and modify the `Next` and `hasNext` methods accordingly.

Although iterators are generally linked to collection style data structures, they can also be used to generate sequences. In the case of a collection, the Next method retrieves the next item in the collection, but for a sequence it simply computes the next value.

For example a CountToTen class would be something like:

```
class CountToTen():Iterator<Int>{
    private var i:Int=1
    override fun next(): Int {
        return i++
    }
    override fun hasNext(): Boolean {
        if(i>10) return false
          return true
    }
}
```

and it could be used anywhere you needed the sequence of numbers. For example:

```
val a=CountToTen()
for(e in a) println(e)
```

prints 1 to 10.

In most cases it would be better to create a class that implemented the Iterable interface. This has just one operator method, iterator, which returns an Iterator object for the class in question.

Notice that an iterator is "lazy" in the sense that it doesn't compute the complete sequence of values at once, it only computes a value when needed. Kotlin has a lot of facilities for functional programming and in functional programming you often chain together functions like iterators which produce sequences.

For efficiency, it is important that these put off creating a sequence until it is actually needed – i.e. they need to be lazy in an extended sense. Kotlin provides the Sequence<T> type to allow you to use and implement iterators that are lazy in this broader sense.

Sequences

Although functional programming isn't the focus of this book, it is worth giving an example of the way iterators and sequences differ, if only because non-functional programmers find it hard to understand why there are two so closely related types.

Compare:

```
val s= sequenceOf( 1,2,3,4,5,6,7,8,9,10 )
val ms=s.map({println(it);it})
println("end")
```

which uses a sequence and:

```
val i= listOf(1,2,3,4,5,6,7,8,9,10)
val mi=i.map({println(it);it})
println("end")
```

which uses the iterator associated with the List.

The map method simply applies the specified function, i.e. the println, to each of the elements of the sequence or collection. If you run this you will discover that the map acting on the sequence doesn't print anything, but the List iterator does. The reason is that in the case of the sequence, map returns an unevaluated sequence ready for further operations. In the case of the List, the map returns another List after evaluating everything. If you want to force the sequence to evaluate, you have to do something that makes use of its results.

For example:

```
val s= sequenceOf( 1,2,3,4,5,6,7,8,9,10 )
val ms=s.map({println(it);it})
println("end")
println(ms.last())
```

You will now see printed:

```
end
1
2
3
4
5
6
7
8
9
10
10
```

This unexpected order of events, i.e. the map happens after the "end" happens because the map isn't evaluated until it is actually needed. So the assignment to `ms` doesn't evaluate the `map`, it is simply stored ready to be evaluated when needed. Then "end" is printed and then the `map` is finally evaluated as its last element is needed. The evaluation is even more lazy than you might imagine in that that if you use `first` in place of `last` then only the first element is evaluated. The lazy evaluation is only performed to the point where the element that is actually needed becomes available.

This is aggressively lazy and it has to be to ensure that many functional forms of simple algorithms are practical.

Ranges & Progressions

Kotlin provides two data types that make it easier to write `for` loops – the `Range` and the `Progression`.

Roughly speaking, `Range` allows you to write things like:

```
for(i in 1..10)
```

and a `Progression` is a range for which you can specify a step size. For example:

```
for(i in 1..10 step 2)
```

As already explained, in connection with the `for` loop, ranges and progressions integrate into the `for` using the `rangeTo` function as an operator `..` and the `step` function.

It isn't difficult to create your own ranges and progressions.

As an example let's create a range that works for dates.

In Java there are far too many date classes in use at the moment, so for simplicity we will use the original `Date` class, despite most of its methods being deprecated. To use this in a Kotlin project you need to add:

```
import java.util.*
```

To create a date range class we need to implement a class, `DateRange`, that implements the `Iterable` interface, and the `ClosedRange` interface which has the `endInclusive` property:

```
class DateRange(override val start: Date,
    override val endInclusive:Date):Iterable<Date>,ClosedRange<Date>
```

We need to add the override modifier to the constructor because the properties created by the primary constructor are hiding properties inherited from `ClosedRange`.

We also have to implement `iterator` which returns a suitable iterator for the range:

```
class DateRange(override val start: Date,
    override val endInclusive:Date):Iterable<Date>,ClosedRange<Date>{
    override fun iterator(): Iterator<Date> {
     return DateRangeIterator(start,endInclusive)
    }
}
```

where `DateRangeIterator` is the iterator we have yet to implement.

`DateRangeIterator` inherits from `Iterator` and `ClosedRange`. We only need to override the iterator's `next` and `hasNext` methods and provide implementations of the `ClosedRange` start and `endInclusive` properties:

```
class DateRangeIterator(val start: Date,
                val endInclusive: Date): Iterator<Date> {
    private var current=start
    override fun next(): Date {
        var next = Date(current.getTime())
        current.setTime(current.getTime() + 24*60*60*1000)
        return next
    }
    override fun hasNext(): Boolean {
        if(current>endInclusive) return false
        return true
    }
}
```

Notice that as `Date` is an object we can't just use:

```
var next=current
```

because `next` and `current` would both reference the same object and changes made to `current` would also change `next`. To keep the values separate, we have to create a new instance with the same values – i.e. we have to clone `current`.

To make the `..` operator work we also need to define a suitable `rangeTo` function:

```
operator fun Date.rangeTo(other: Date) = DateRange(this, other)
```

With this all defined, all that remains is to use the new range class:

```
val dfm = SimpleDateFormat("yyyy-MM-dd")
val startDay=dfm.parse("2017-01-01")
val endDay=dfm.parse("2017-01-07")
  for(d in startDay..endDay){
       println(d)
  }
```

which prints:

```
Sun Jan 01 00:00:00 GMT 2017
Mon Jan 02 00:00:00 GMT 2017
Tue Jan 03 00:00:00 GMT 2017
Wed Jan 04 00:00:00 GMT 2017
Thu Jan 05 00:00:00 GMT 2017
Fri Jan 06 00:00:00 GMT 2017
Sat Jan 07 00:00:00 GMT 2017
```

What about adding a `step` function to turn it into a progression?

This is easy, because all we really need to do is provide a step parameter and an implementation of the `step` infix operator. The way that this works is fairly simple. If we have a `for` loop:

```
for(d in startDay..endDay step 2){
      println(d)
   }
```

Then the `rangeTo` function is called with `startDay` and `endDay` and this creates a Range object, i.e. a Progression object with a step size of 1. Next the `step` infix operator is called on the object that the `rangeTo` function returned i.e. range.step(2) and this has to use the `Range` object to construct a `Progression` object with the same start and end dates and a step size as specified.

If we were creating the `Progression` class "properly" then we would implement it as a class, and the `Range` class would inherit from it – after all what is a `Range` but a `Progression` with step=1.

For simplicity let's just modify the code that we have for `Range` and turn it into a `Progression` in all but name.

First we need to update the `DataRangeIterator` to use a step parameter:

```
class DateRangeIterator(val start: Date,
      val endInclusive: Date, val step: Long) : Iterator<Date> {
   private var current = start
   override fun hasNext(): Boolean {
    if (current > endInclusive) return false
    return true
   }
   override fun next(): Date {
    var next = Date(current.getTime())
    current.setTime(current.getTime() + step * 24 * 60 * 60 * 1000)
    return next
   }
}
```

Notice that `step` is specified in days.

With this change we need to modify the `DataRange` class to set the new `step` parameter:

```
class DateRange(override val start: Date,
                override val endInclusive: Date,
                val step: Long = 1) : Iterable<Date>,
                                      ClosedRange<Date> {
    override fun iterator(): Iterator<Date> {
        return DateRangeIterator(start, endInclusive, step)
    }
}
```

Notice that the default value of 1 for the `step` parameter means that this can be called to create a range without a step argument at all. The `rangeTo` function stays the same:

```
operator fun Date.rangeTo(other: Date) = DateRange(this, other)
```

where the `DataRange` object still has a step size of 1. It is not until we define the `step` infix operator that it is modified to have a different step size.

The step infix operator function is:

```
infix fun DateRange.step(step: Long): DateRange {
    return DateRange(this.start,this.endInclusive,step)
}
```

This is called on the `DateRange` object that the `rangeTo` creates, and is used to construct a new `DateRange` object, but this time with a step size that is something other than 1. In a more general setting this would create an instance of a more appropriate class, a `DateProgression` say, but there is no real difference in implementation from the poorly named `DateRange`.

Now we can write:

```
val dfm = SimpleDateFormat("yyyy-MM-dd")
    val startDay = dfm.parse("2017-01-01")
    val endDay = dfm.parse("2017-01-07")
    for (d in startDay..endDay step 2) {
        println(d)
    }
```

which produces

```
Sun Jan 01 00:00:00 GMT 2017
Tue Jan 03 00:00:00 GMT 2017
Thu Jan 05 00:00:00 GMT 2017
Sat Jan 07 00:00:00 GMT 2017
```

There are lots of things missing from this implementation of a `Progression` object – there are no checks for a positive step size, and there are lots of missing methods – downTo, reversed and so on – but it does illustrate how flexible the implementation of the Kotlin `for` loop can be.

Summary

- Collections store objects as references and make use of generics to work with any type of object.

- The base class is `Collection`, but `List` and `MutableList` are the best examples of how collections work.

- Collections generally have factory methods such as `collectionOf` to create initialized instances. Some also make use of their constructor and an initialization function.

- Kotlin collections come in mutable and immutable versions. The immutable version is more like a read-only type than a truly immutable data structure.

- The other core collection types are maps and sets. `Map` stores key value/pairs. `Set` stores objects in no particular order without duplicates.

- An iterator is an object with at least two methods – `next`, which returns the next object, and `hasNext`, which is `true` if there is a `next` object.

- Iterators are used to implement `for` loops and other basic Kotlin constructs and you can implement custom iterators.

- Sequences are lazy iterators designed to make functional programming in Kotlin more efficient.

- `Range` is a special sort of iterator that has a `start` and `stop` value.

- `Progression` is a range with a step size, `step`.

- You can implement custom ranges and progressions.

Chapter 10

Advanced Functions

Although we have had a brief look at functions in an earlier chapter, functions are so central to what makes Kotlin special that they deserve a chapter to themselves. In this chapter we look at how functions make Kotlin more powerful and easier to use.

Free Functions

In languages such as Java, functions don't really exist outside objects. In fact, you could say that in Java there are no functions, only methods. Of course, this has started to change recently and Java now has lambda functions, which can be regarded as functions that don't belong to an object.

Kotlin is much freer than Java in the way you can use functions and it has lots of features that are only now making their way into newer versions of Java. Even so, Kotlin manages to map these more advanced features back onto the earlier versions of Java and this causes some compromises.

Although we have covered the basic facts of functions in Chapter 2, it is worth gathering things together and presenting a more complete picture in this chapter. Variations on Kotlin's basic functions - anonymous, lambda and inline functions - are covered in the next chapter.

It is probably true to say that it is Kotlin's rich and varied modifications and additions to the basic idea of a function that makes it so attractive. However, many of the features are almost ad-hoc adaptions to fit in with the way that functions are used. This can make it seem difficult to see the overall logic.

In addition, code that takes full advantage of the most concise mode of expression using functions can become very difficult to understand. This is particularly true when we meet expression functions in the next chapter.

Functions & Methods

Kotlin supports both functions and functions as methods.

To define a function you use:

```
fun name(parameters){ body of function }
```

You can also specify a return type after the closing parenthesis. If you don't specify a return type, `Unit` is assumed. A function with a body and a return type has to have a return statement.

If the body only has a single expression, the function can be written more simply as:

```
fun name(parameters)= expression
```

Again the return type is optional if it can be inferred.

The only surface difference between a function and a method is that a method definition is associated with a class and, when used, with an instance of that class. A function, on the other hand, isn't associated with a class or an instance of a class.

Functions can be defined at the package level, i.e. not within a class, or they can be defined within other functions, including within methods.

Of course all of this is a sleight of hand. To remain compatible with Java, top level functions are implemented in a static class with a name `packagename.filename` where `filename` is the name of the file including the `Kt` extension.

So, if a hello world was stored in a file called `Hello.kt`, the class is `demo.HelloKt`, assuming the package is called `demo`.

This means that the first thing that a new Kotlin programmer encounters is a top level function called `main` with no sign of the customary static class so familiar in Java. This is just syntactic sugar as the `main` function is indeed a member of a static class with the same name as the package and file. You can change the name of the static class using an annotation, see Chapter 13:

```
@file:JvmName("class name")
```

As a consequence of this implementation method, you can see that top-level functions and methods are the same thing under the skin, and any feature you can use with one you can use with the other.

Local functions, however, are a little different. They are not accessible outside the containing function, and they have access to the containing function's variables, but it doesn't have access to theirs. This is exactly what you would expect from a local entity. For example, you can have a local block of code:

```
fun myMethod(){
 var a=0
 {
  println(a)
  var b=0
 }
 println(b)
}
```

where a is accessible within the block, but b isn't accessible outside the block and so the println(b) fails. Notice that a block of code acts like a function that you don't have to call – it is a manually implemented inline function, see the next chapter.

The same holds for a local function:

```
var a=0
fun myFunction(){
     var b=0
     println(a)
 }
 myFunction()
 println(b)
}
```

In this case the println(a) works, as the local function has access to the containing functions variables and parameters but the println(b) fails because the containing function cannot access any variables or parameters of the local function. Also notice that you can't call a local function before it has been declared.

Local functions are useful when a function or a method grows too big. Methods and functions should never have more than a few tens of lines of code, but often the idea of breaking a method up into utility functions doesn't fit in with the rest of the structure. The answer is to split the method into a number of local functions, which only it can call. In this way the method gets its own private utility function library.

Local functions are implemented as anonymous classes with a single method that corresponds to the function. In Java, and hence for any language that compiles to the JVM, a function is always part of a class and hence is a method. The Kotlin compiler hides this from you and most of the time it doesn't matter. The only time it does matter is if efficiency is an issue. In this case you need to consider using inline functions – see the next chapter.

Parameters

Functions have parameters and Kotlin functions have more sophisticated parameters than many languages, but first we need to look at the basic way that they work.

In Kotlin all parameters are passed by value, as is the case in Java.

What this means is that if you pass a variable to a function, the value it contains is converted into a local, read-only, copy. This has a number of consequences. The first is that you cannot use a parameter to pass a result back from a function. In fact you cannot change a parameter's value within a function as it is treated as a `val` and is read-only.

If you pass a variable that references an object, then the reference is passed by value, and within the function the parameter references the same object. What this means is that you cannot change the parameter within the function – it is still read-only. But you can change properties of the object that it references.

For example:

```
class MyClass(var myProperty: Int=0){...
fun myFunction(myObject: MyClass) {
    myObject.myProperty = 1
    }
val myObjectA = MyClass()
myFunction(myObjectA)
```

Notice that `myFunction` changes `myProperty`, which makes it look as if the object has been passed by reference, and in a weak sense it has.

Notice also that you can use a reference to an object to get results out of a function, but generally this isn't a good idea. Use a data object to collect the multiple values as properties and return it if you need multiple results. If you put this together with destructuring it looks exactly like a function that has multiple results.

To summarize:

- All parameters are passed by value.
- Parameters are read-only val types.
- Object references are passed as read-only values referencing the same object.
- This means you can change properties on an object from within a function – this isn't a good idea.

Default, Named & Variable Parameters

Let's go through the possible variations on simple parameters in order of increasing sophistication.

If you simply specify some parameters then you always have to specify their type as there is no way the system can infer this until the function is used:

```
fun myFunction(p1:Int,p2:String,p3:MyClass){
}
```

Default parameters

You can provide default values for parameters, but you still to specify the type, even if this could be inferred:

```
fun myFunction(p1:Int=0,p2:String="abc",p3:MyClass=MyClass()){
}
```

Default values allow you to leave out parameters, and this means you don't have to implement an overloaded function for each subset of parameters you want to support.

However, Kotlin doesn't provide any way of indicating omitted parameters, so you can't use a default for parameter 1 and then specify a value for parameter 2. The first parameter you specify is always parameter 1. What this means is that you need to put default parameters at the end of the list of parameters.

Once the call uses a default parameter it uses all of the remaining parameters as defaults.

For example:

```
fun sum(a:Int=0,b:Int){return a+b}
```

calling this with sum(1) sets a to 1. There is no way to make it set b to 1 while accepting the default for a.

If you have a method with default parameters then it can be overridden, but you can't change the defaults and you don't specify them in the redefinition. That is, the new function has the same defaults as the old function.

If you call a function with defaults from Java, you have to call the function with all parameters used, i.e. you cannot rely on the defaults.

Named parameters

The problem with specifying default parameter values with only positional parameters leads us on to the next variation - named parameters. You don't have to do anything extra, you simply use the parameters as if they were variables within the function call.

For example:

```
myFunction(p3=MyClass(),p1=1)
```

sets values for the first and third parameters and the second takes its default value.

Using named parameters in this way not only makes it possible to be selective about which parameters use their defaults, it also makes function calls more understandable, but only if you give parameters sensible, meaningful names, which is usually a difficult task.

Variable parameters

The final parameter trick that Kotlin has for us is variable argument lists.

The basic idea is that one of the parameters can be marked as a vararg. You can only have one vararg parameter and it is usually the last. The reason is that when the vararg parameter begins accepting values it continues until the closing parenthesis is reached. This means that the only way to set any parameters beyond the vararg is by name. The values stored in the vararg are treated as an array of the indicated type. Notice that a vararg can only be of a single type and its sub-types. You can think of vararg as an instruction to pack all of the arguments that follow into an array.

For example:

```
 fun myFunction(vararg va:Int){
    println(va[0])
    println(va[1])
  }
```

Of course it is up to you to make sure that you don't try and use an array element that doesn't exist. You can use generics with vararg but of course this restricts what you can do with the parameters. If you want to allow mixed parameters then you can also use Any and casts:

```
fun myFunction(vararg va:Any){
    println(va[0] )
    println(va[1])
  }
myFunction(1,"abc",3,4)
```

This & Methods

When you call a method:

```
myObject.myMethod(parameters)
```

this is an alternative way of writing:

```
myMethod(myObject,parameters)
```

That is, the object instance the method is called on, is conceptually the same as an additional parameter.

The additional parameter is usually named `this` and it is referred to as the receiver or the call context and of course, it isn't passed as parameter, it is just made available within the object.

In most cases you don't have to use `this` within the method to refer to the instance, because it is assumed that your references are to the current instance.

For example if you are writing a class.

```
class MyClass{
 var myProperty:Int=0
 fun myMethod(){
  myProperty=1
 }
}
```

the reference to `myProperty` in `myMethod` is shorthand for:

```
this.myProperty
```

but as it within the class declaration it is assumed. Sometimes it is a good idea to explicitly write `this` to distinguish what is and what is not a member of the class.

For example:

```
class MyClass{
 var myProperty:Int=0
 fun myMethod(myProperty:Int){
  this.myProperty=myProperty
 }
}
```

You have to write `this.myProperty` to distinguish it from the `myProperty` parameter. In most cases this isn't necessary.

Qualified this

As already stated, you can think of this as an extra parameter that is set to reference the object that the method is currently working with. This is standard across most object-oriented programming languages, but Kotlin goes a little further.

In Kotlin you can have inner classes, and this means that in a method you can have an inner and an outer context. The same applies to extension functions and function literals with a receiver – see the next chapter.

Normally this refers to the innermost enclosing scope, i.e. the object you would most expect it to refer to. You can make this reference an outer scope by using a label. By default classes have labels that use the same name as the class.

A simple example is difficult to construct because, at the least, you need one inner class:

```
class MyOuterClass(var myProperty: Int = 0) {
 inner class MyInnerClass(var myProperty: Int = 1) {
    fun myInnerMethod() {
      println(this.myProperty)
      println(this@MyInnerClass.myProperty)
      println(this@MyOuterClass.myProperty)
    }
    }
    fun MyOuterMethod(){
        val myInnerObject=MyInnerClass()
        myInnerObject.myInnerMethod()
    }
}
```

In this case we have an outer class with an inner class which has a property of the same name as the outer class and a single method that prints this.myProperty, this@MyInnerClass.myProperty and this@MyOuterClass.myProperty.

To try this out we need an instance of the outer class:

```
var myObject = MyOuterClass()
myObject.MyOuterMethod()
```

What you see is 1,1,0 corresponding to the inner class's property twice, followed by the outer class's property.

This is a potentially very confusing, but occasionally useful, feature of the language.

Extension Functions

In Kotlin you can add a method to any class without needing access to the class declaration. This seems to be almost magic, but if you keep in mind the way that methods and this works it seems simple.

An extension method discovers the instance it is to work with via this, which is set to reference the instance or receiver when the method is called. Methods get their this parameter by virtue of being part of a class, but any function that has access to a parameter that provides a reference to the current instance can look like a class member, even if it isn't.

Kotlin provides the this mechanism to any function, even if it isn't a member of the class – it simply has to be declared in association with the class.

For example:

```
fun MyClass.myExtension(){
  this.myProperty=1
  this.myMethod()
}
```

myExtension is not part of MyClass but it can now be called as if it was:

```
val myObject=MyClass()
myObject.myExtension()
```

It looks as if myExtension is a method of myObject but of course it isn't. The call:

```
myObject.myExtension()
```

is equivalent to:

```
myExtension(myObject)
```

where this is the first parameter of the function call. This is a simple syntactic change.

Notice that this implies that the extension method has no access to the internal workings of the class, only its public methods and properties.

You might think that this would limit the usefulness of extension methods, but the ability to add methods to classes that you don't have access to, including built-in classes such as Int and String, is so useful that the Kotlin standard library has lots of extension methods.

Extension methods can, of course, be generic.

Now we come to the question of how the compiler knows that there is a suitable extension?

Suppose we have two extensions:

```
fun MyClassA.myExtension(){...}
```

and:

```
fun MyClassB:myExtension{...}
```

and you write:

```
val myObjectB=MyClassB()
myObjectB.myExtension()
```

The compiler knows that there is an extension method called `myExtension` for `MyClassA` and `MyClassB` and obviously it selects the one defined on `MyClassB` to call for `myObjectB`.

The important point is that it is the type of the variable at compile time that determines which extension function is called. That is, extensions are resolved statically at compile type rather than dynamically at run time.
To see why this matters consider the situation where `MyClassB` is a subclass of MyClassA. Now if we try:

```
var myObject:MyClassA
myObject=MyClassB()
```

which is fine, as `MyClassB` can be treated as if it was a `MyClassA`. We now have a variable of type `MyClassA` referencing an object of type `MyClassB` and the question is, which extension method will be called using:

```
myObject.myExtension()
```

The answer is, the one that was defined on `MyClassA`, because this is the type of the variable and extension methods are resolved statically on the type of the variable they are called on.

Notice that this is true of a generic extension method:

```
fun <T>  mutableList<T>.myExtension(){..}
myObject.myExtension()
```

will call the extension with < Int > if the `myObject` variable is of type `mutableList<Int>` , irrespective of any variance.

There are also some general points to keep in mind. Extension methods cannot be local, but they can be methods of another class. In this case, `this` resolves both to the instance of the class that the extension is a method of, and to the instance of the class it extends as required. If there is any doubt about which `this` is to be used you can use `this@MyClass` or `this@MyExtensionClass`.

Extension methods can be overridden in subclasses, and which extension method is used is dynamic, i.e. virtual, on the class the extension is a member of, and static on the class it extends.

Also, if a class has a member function with the same signature, then it is called in preference to the extension function. You can define extension functions that have the same name as a member, but the signatures have to be different.

If you are extending a nullable type you have to make sure to check for this being null in the extension.

As a property is just a special case of a function member, that is a property is just a pair of `get` and `set` functions, you can have extension properties. However, as extension functions do not have access to the class, they cannot have backing fields, and hence cannot be initialized. An extension property is therefore limited to computing a value using other functions and other properties of the class.

For example:
```
val String.lastChar:Char
get()= this[length-1]
```
retrieves the last character in any string and you can use it as if it was a normal String property, e.g:
```
val myString="abcde"
println(myString.lastChar)
```
You can also define extension methods for companion objects, i.e. static extension methods. You define the method using the name of the companion object:
```
MyClass.Companion.myExtension(){}
```
and call it as if it was a normal "static" method of the class:
```
MyClass.myExtension()
```

Infix Functions

A very nice and very simple syntactic transformation is to convert:

```
object1 function object2
```

into

```
object1.function(object2)
```

This allows you to write functions as infix operators.

This only works for methods and extension functions, because it has to be possible to call the function with a sensible this value. It also only works with functions with a single parameter.

For example, we can define an infix extension function's sum:

```
infix fun Int.sum(a:Int):Int {
  return this+a
}
```

Now we can write:

```
1 sum 2
```

and get the result 3.

It is obvious, from the fact that you can use a function call in an expression, that infix functions can be used in expressions in a natural manner.

For example:

```
1 sum 2 * 3
```

is 7 as multiplication has a higher priority than a function call.

Function Types

In most cases all you really need to know is the signature of a function, i.e. what the types are of its parameters, and perhaps its return type. The signature of a function is used to determine which function is called if there are a number of overloads.

Sometimes, however, we need to define a type that corresponds to a particular signature and return type. For this we need to create a specific function type.

For example:

```
(String)->Int
```

defines a function type that takes a `String` and returns an `Int`.

Similarly:

```
(Int,Int)->Int
```

defines a function type that takes two `Int`s and returns an `Int`. As already introduced in Chapter 7 we can define a type alias to avoid having to type out a function type definition each time it is needed.

For example:

```
typealias arith =(Int,Int)->Int
```

defines the `arith` type to be a function that takes two `Int`s and returns an `Int`.

The only not-quite-obvious function type is:

```
()->Unit
```

which is the type of a function taking no parameters and returning no result.

Summary

- Kotlin gives the impression that you can define functions outside of classes i.e. functions that are not methods, but in fact it converts these into methods of a default class.

- You can set the name of the default class using:

  `@file:JvmName("class name")`

- Local functions can access the containing functions variables but not vice versa.

- All parameters are passed by value and are read-only `val` types.

- As object references are passed as read-only values, referencing the this object means you can change properties on an object from within a function.

- You can also use default, named and `vararg` parameters.

- The receiver or call context is represented by `this` in methods.

- For nested classes `this` can be qualified by the name for the class for which the call context is required.

- Extension functions can make use of `this` to make them look as if they are methods of an existing class, but they cannot access the internal workings of the class.

- Methods and extension functions with a single parameter can be used as infix operators with the object to the left as the call context, and the object on the right as the single parameter.

- You can define a function type as the signature and return type of the function.

Chapter 11

Anonymous, Lambdas & Inline Functions

Languages that don't allow functions to exist as entities in their own right make things difficult without many advantages. Kotlin introduces features to allow functions to be treated in more flexible ways, in particular to be used as parameters to other functions. In this chapter we look at anonymous functions, function references, lambda functions and inline functions.

Many of Kotlin's language innovations are about how you can use functions. As well as being able to use standalone "classical" functions, Kotlin also provides function expression and references, which allow you to pass functions to other functions. One of the problems is that this has resulted in a confusing menagerie of new and different function types.

When it comes to functions in Kotlin, there is usually more than one way to get a particular job done.

Anonymous Functions & References

What isn't as well known as it should be, is that you can create a variable of a function type and you can store a reference to a function in it.

For example:

```
typealias arith=(Int,Int)->Int

var myfunc:arith
myfunc=fun(a:Int,b:Int):Int{return a+b}

println(myfunc(1,2))
```

Notice that the function isn't anything new like a lambda function, it is just a standard function that doesn't have a name – an anonymous function.

An anonymous function is just like any other function and can have named parameters, default values and so on. The only real difference is that it doesn't have a name and so can't be invoked in the usual way. However, you can store a reference to it in a variable of the correct type and invoke it using the usual () operator.

What is even less well known is that you can use a named function in the same way, i.e. as a function reference.

141

You can't simply assign a named function to a variable of the correct type because Kotlin demands that, if you just use the name of a function, you are invoking it and have to provide arguments and handle the return type.

For example, if you try:

```
var myfunc:arith
fun sum(a:Int,b:Int):Int{return a+b}
myfunc=sum
```

you will get an error message saying that you haven't invoked the function with arguments, i.e the compiler is expecting sum(1,2) or similar.

However, if you make use of the :: reflection reference operator then you can obtain a reference to the function.

That is:

```
var myfunc:arith
fun sum(a:Int,b:Int):Int{return a+b}
myfunc=::sum
```

works and it does store a reference to sum in myfunc which can then be used to call the function:

```
println(myfunc(1,2))
```

You can pass an anonymous function as an argument to another function and using the :: operator you can pass a reference to a named function in the same way.

For example if you define a function which accepts an arith function type, executes it, and prints the result:

```
fun myfuncDisplay(a:arith){
        println(a(1,2))
}
```

then you can call it and pass the anonymous myfunc:

```
myfuncDisplay(myfunc)
```

or the named sum function:

```
myfuncDisplay(::sum)
```

Lambda Functions

The usual reason for introducing lambda functions into a language is to allow functions to be treated as more like first class citizens in the language. In the case of Kotlin we already have the ability to store and pass references to both named and anonymous functions.

In this case lambdas mostly provide a more compact way to define functions.

The key difference between a named or anonymous function and a lambda function is that a lambda is treated as an expression which can be invoked using the () operator.

A lambda function can be declared using the arrow operator -> within curly brackets. On the left of the arrow you list the parameters, and on the right you list the code that works with the parameters.

Notice that you cannot specify a return type for a lambda – it has to be deduced by type inference.

That is a lambda is:

```
{ parameter list -> code }
```

The code can either be a single expression or a multi-line body and the last value computed is returned as the value of the function.

For example, we could write the anonymous sum function introduced in the previous section as:

```
var sum={a:Int,b:Int -> a+b}
```

where we are relying on type inference for the type of sum and hence the return type.

You can call sum in the usual way:

```
sum(1,2)
```

However, lambdas are usually passed as parameters to other functions and tend to be defined as needed rather than stored.

Lambdas & Anonymous Functions As Extensions

You can define both lambda and anonymous functions as extensions and they work in the same way.

For example:

```
val sum=fun Int.(other:Int):Int {return this+other}
```

defines an anonymous function that is an extension method of Int called using:

```
1.sum(2)
```

If you want to use a lambda in this way you have to supply the type:

```
val sum: Int.(Int)->Int= {other:Int-> this+other}
```

and it can be called in exactly the same way:

```
1.sum(2)
```

You can pass a lambda extension in the same way, by specifying a function type:

```
fun myEvaluate(f:Int.(Int)->Int):Int{
        return 1.f(2)
}
```

Now you can call `myEvaluate` with a lambda-like syntax:

```
myEvaluate({other:Int->this+other})
```

or more simply:

```
myEvaluate {other:Int->this+other}
```

As the documentation explains, this can be used to create type-safe builders.

DSLs & Metaprogramming

A syntactic simplification is that if the last parameter of a function is itself a function, then it can be passed outside of the usual parameter parenthesis.

For example, if we have:

```
fun myFunction(p1,p2,function)
```

you can call `myFunction` using:

```
myFunction(p1,p2) { code for the function}
```

which is exactly the same as:

```
myFunction(p1,p2,{code for the function})
```

If the function has no other parameters at all then you can even leave out the parentheses. For example:

```
myFunction {code for the function}
```

is the same as:

```
myFunction({code for the function})
```

Why are any of these syntactic changes useful?

The answer is that you can make a lambda look like a new construct within the language – i.e. it is good for the construction of Domain Specific Languages, DSLs.

For example, if you want to add a simple `Repeat`(n) loop, which repeats a block of code n times this is easy:

```
fun myRepeat(count:Int ,body:()->Unit){
    var i:Int=0
    while(i<count){
        i++
        body()
      }
}
```

144

Because of the syntax rule that you can place a final function parameter outside of the parenthesis this can be used in a way that makes it look like a new Kotlin control structure:

```
myRepeat(10){
        println("Hello World")
    }
```

which prints "Hello World" ten times.

This is the sort of facility you can waste hours on, designing neat ways of implementing custom features that aren't really essential. It also has some limitations.

For example, to implement a custom while loop you would need to pass two parameters – a conditional expression of function and a body of code, and this cannot be treated in the same neat way.

No Local Return

A surprising restriction is that you can't use return in a lambda function. A return always returns from a function defined using fun and this is something that is enforced by the JVM. Lambda functions in Kotlin are not implemented in this way and hence you cannot use return.

You can, however, use a qualified return which behaves more like a goto command. The problem with a qualified return is that, because a lambda definition is so short, there isn't a sensible location to label.

The best you can do is something like:

```
var max = lambda@{ a: Int, b: Int ->
        if (a > b) return@lambda a
        return@lambda b
    }
```

which works but isn't a particularly clear expression of what is happening. Notice that this function is much better written as:

```
var max:Int =  {a: Int, b: Int ->
        if (a > b)  a else b
    }
```

where the if is interpreted as an if expression returning either a or b.

It is worth knowing at this early stage that you can use a return in an inlined lambda function, see later.

Compact Lambdas, it, _ & IIFE

One of the aspects of lambdas that can be confusing is how compact they can be. For example if there are no parameters you can simply omit them. So:

```
{1+2}
```

is a lambda that returns the result of 1+2, i.e. 3

The very simplest lambda is just a single value which by default is its return value:

```
{0}
```

which is a lambda that returns 0.

If your lambda has a single parameter, you also don't need to explicitly provide it in the definition, as the compiler will assume that any use of a variable named it in in the body is a single parameter.

For example:

```
var d={it*2}
```

is a single parameter lambda that returns the parameter times two and you would call it using;

```
println(d(2))
```

You can also leave out a parameter in a lambda if it isn't going to be used by replacing it with an underscore. This is useful when you have another function that calls the lambda with more parameters than you care to use.

For example the arith type demands that any lambda that conforms has two int parameters:

```
typealias arith =(Int,Int)->Int
```

If we want to write an arith lambda that only uses the second parameter we can write:

```
var neg:arith={_,b->-b}
```

this still conforms to the arith type, even though it only uses one parameter. Of course, you could simply include a dummy parameter and then ignore it, but this form at least makes it clear that you are only using a single parameter.

Notice that these expressions are functions and to return a value they have to be invoked. You can call a lambda immediately after it has been defined – a so called Immediately-Invoked Function Expression or IIFE.

For example:

```
var sum={1+2}()
```

sets sum not to a function but to 3. Similarly:

```
 var max:Int =  {a: Int, b: Int ->
        if (a > b)  a else b
    }(1,2)
println(max)
```

prints 2 and you do have to supply the type of max as the compiler can't work it out for you.

You can IIFE any lambda function, but you cannot IIFE a named or anonymous function because they are not expressions.

Closure

Closure is one of the most mystifying aspects of lambdas. The Kotlin documentation makes a lot of the fact that a lambda has access to the local variables of any function that encloses it, but this is really just the way that local variable work rather than closure.

Closure, in the way that most languages implement it, means having access to variables that were local but are no longer in scope. The simplest example of this is when a function returns a lambda. While the function is executing, the lambda has access to variables that are local to the function – but not only this, it has access to them when the function has completed and the local variables have been, in principle, destroyed. You can think of this as the lambda "capturing" the variables in a closure.

Kotlin supports this sort of closure. For example, if we define a function that returns a simple lambda:

```
fun myFunction():()->Unit{
    var a=1
    var lambda= {println(a);a=a+1}
    return lambda
}
```

There are several interesting things about this function. The first is that its return type is ()->Unit, i.e. it returns a function that accepts no parameters and returns nothing, i.e. Unit. This is indeed the type of the lambda it returns. The lambda in question simply prints the value of a and adds one to it. Note that a is a local variable in myFunction and it is only accessible from within myFunction and it is destroyed when myFunction returns, i.e. it normally only exists while myFunction is active.

If you now call myFunction to get an instance of the lambda:

```
var mylambda=myFunction()
```

and then call the lambda twice:

```
    mylambda()
    mylambda()
```

what do you think will happen?

The answer is that it prints 1 followed by 2. The instance has access to the local variable that should have been destroyed when myFunction terminated, and it not only has access to its initial value but it can modify it.

It is important to realize that each time you return a new instance of the lambda the local variable a is a new local variable.

For example:

```
var mylambda1=myFunction()
var mylambda2=myFunction()
mylambda1()
mylambda1()
mylambda2()
mylambda2()
```

You will see 1,2 and then 1,2 printed because the variable a captured by mylambda1 is not the same as the a captured by mylambda2.

Closure works with named and anonymous functions as well as pure lambda functions. In the case of named functions it has to be a local function and you have to use the :: operator.

For example:

```
fun myFunction():()->Unit{
    var a=1
    fun namedFunction(){
        println(a)
        a=a+1
    }
    var lambda= ::namedFunction
    return lambda
}
```

If you are unfamiliar with lambda functions or functions as first class objects you might be wondering what use closure is?

There are a number of standard uses of closure, but perhaps the most useful is when you are defining an event handler of a callback function. Lambdas and anonymous functions make supplying a callback very easy. However, the callback is usually designed to process the end result of some long running task and this usually involves the function that created the callback. If the task wasn't long running you would have simply waited for it to complete and then processed its return value. The callback breaks up the original function into before the task and after the task. By allowing the callback access to the function's local variables, closure allows a degree of communication between the original function and the callback.

Inline Functions

Functions are good for efficiency in the sense that they allow you to reuse a block of code as many times as you like, but without having to include the code multiple times in your program. However, functions are also bad for efficiency in that each Kotlin function creates an object to host each one, and the need to create a closure also slows things down. There are overheads in using a function as well as advantages.

An alternative way of implementing functions is for the compiler to essentially copy the code of the function into any location it is called. For example if you call the sum function:

```
var ans=sum(1,2)
```

then the compiler would convert this into the equivalent:

```
var ans=1+2
```

There is no trace of the function in the generated code. The compiler simply copies the code in the function to the call location and removes the function call and return – after all there is no function to return from any more.

Of course, a real function would most likely have tens of lines of instructions and these would be copied and hence duplicated in the compiled code each time the function was called. It might make your application larger but it is often worth the trade off.

In Kotlin you can ask the compiler to inline a function using the inline modifier. Notice that you can only inline named functions and not anonymous or lambda functions – however, functions passed to inline are inlined. This is an important point and you could say that the whole point of inlining is to remove the expense of passing functions into other functions.

For example:

```
inline fun sum(a:Int,b:int){
  return a+b
}
```

Now when you call sum the function isn't called in the usual way and the return is removed as there is nothing to return from. If you try this function out the compiler will generate a warning that it is far to simple a function to bother inlining. You can take its advice or ignore it.

This would be the end of the story but inlining code creates a number of differences between a standard function and an inlined function.

149

The most basic is that an inline function cannot call itself and it cannot call a function that in turn calls it. If you understand how inline functions are implemented you will see why this is so. At run time there is no function to call.

Inlining a function will cause the compiler to inline any functions that are passed to it via its parameters. If you don't want a passed function to be inlined then you can use the `noinline` modifier.

For example:

```
inline fun myfuncDisplay(noinline a:arith){
        println(a(1,2))
    }
```

will inline the call to `myfunc` but not the passed `arith` function.

You can also inline properties that don't have backing fields – both the `get` and `put` or just one of them. All you have to do is put inline in front of the property or the getter or setter of your choice. The `get` or `set` function is inlined in the usual way. The reason you can't use a backing property is that the inline code is generated outside of the class/object and so the inline getter and setter cannot access any internal variables.

Non-Local Returns

The biggest impact that inlining has is that any return statements that you include in a lambda will appear in the inline function as if they were returns from it. This sounds complicated, but it is trivial if you keep in mind the re-writing process. When the compiler writes the code of an inline function at the call site it removes any returns - there is nothing to return from. However, when it inlines a lambda parameter it doesn't remove any returns and these are simply placed in the code.

This sometimes produces results that you want and it sometimes doesn't.

It is difficult to find a simple example that is realistic, but consider the following set of functions.

First an `inline` function that accepts a lambda of type `arith`, evaluates it and prints the result:

```
inline fun myEvaluate(f:arith){
    var result=f(1,2)
    println(result)
}
```

Next a `noinline` function which uses `myEvaluate`:

```
fun myNonInline(){
    println("before")
    myEvaluate({a, b -> a+b})
    println("after")
}
```

If we call myNoninline in main:

```
fun main(args: Array<String>) {
    myNonInline()
}
```

you see exactly what you would expect:

```
before
3
after
```

Now try changing the lambda to:

```
fun myNonInline(){
    println("before")
    myEvaluate({a, b -> return a+b})
    println("after")
}
```

i.e. add return in front of the returned value. What you get is an error:

```
fun myNonInline(){
    println("before")
    myEvaluate({a, b -> return a+b})
    println("after")
}                          ┌──────────────────
                           │ Type mismatch.
    }                      │ Required:  Unit
                           │ Found:     Int
    fun main(args: Array<Strir└──────────────────
```

If you are not aware that myEvaluate is an inline function then this is mystifying as myEvaluate is declared as returning an Int - where does the Unit come from?

The answer is that myEvaluate is inlined into the body of myNonInline as is the lambada – including the return. The inlined code is equivalent to:

```
fun myNonInline(){
    println("before")
    var result=return 1+2
    println(result)
    println("after")
}
```

Now you can see where the Unit comes from. The return is a from myNonInline function and it has a Unit return type.

To make this work you have to change myNonInline to return an Int:

```
fun myNonInline():Int{
    println("before")
    myEvaluate({a, b -> return a+b})
    println("after")
    return 1
}
```

151

Now the error message vanishes and you can run the code but what you see might still be surprising. All you see printed is "before". This is perfectly obvious when you know that the code is equivalent to:

```
fun myNonInline():Int{
    println("before")
    var result=return 1+2
    println(result)
    println("after")
    return 1
}
```

Clearly the return 1+2 ends the myNonInline function which you can demonstrate using:

```
println(myNonInline())
```

which prints 3.

A return in an inlined lambda passed to an inlined function is a return from the outer function with uses the inlined function.

As already mentioned sometimes this non-local return behavior is an advantage, but most of the time it isn't.

The example given in the documentation explains that non-local returns are desired behavior in functional loops.

For example:

```
fun hasZeros(ints:List<Int>):Boolean{
 ints.forEach{
   if(it==0) return true
 }
 return false
}
```

In this case forEach is assumed to be an inline function and hence its lambda parameter performs a non-local return which ends the outer noninline function.

Reified Type

The final consequence of inlining a function is the reification on type parameters. Reified means to make real and in this case what appears to be an advanced concept is just another simple consequence of the re-writing involved in an inline function. When you create a standard generic the type that is assigned is lost or erased at run time because all generic parameters are implemented as Any.

What this means is that you cannot write the following simple function:

```
fun <T> IS(obj:Any):Boolean{
    return obj is T
}
```

It should return true or false depending on what type obj and T are. Unfortunately this doesn't work.

This isn't possible at run time because the type of the object is always Any.

We can make it work by reifying the type parameter as part of the inline rewriting process. If you just make the function inline then the generic type will not be reified and you will still be working with an object of type Any. You also have to add reified to the type parameter:

```
inline fun <reified T> IS(obj:Any):Boolean{
    return obj is T
}
```

with these small changes the function works and:

```
IS<Int>("23")
```

returns false but:

```
IS<int>(23)
```

returns true.

If you have a valid reified type parameter T then you can use:

```
obj  is  T
obj !is  T
obj  as  T
Obj  as? T
```

and reflection.

The way that it works is that the type parameter is replaced by the actual type when the inline code is generated.

So at the calling site:

```
IS <Int>(23)
```

becomes:

```
obj is Int
```

which is perfectly valid and works.

Type reification is a small step in the right direction but you have to admit that Kotlin is boxed in by what Java and the JVM allows it to do. However, Java compatibility is well worth the trade off.

Summary

- You can store a reference to an anonymous function in a variable or pass the function as an argument to another function.

- You can store a reference to a named function in a variable or parameter using the reflection reference operator ::

- A reference to a lambda function can also be stored in a variable or passed as a parameter.

- A lambda is defined as `{ parameter list -> code }`

- A lambda, anonymous or named function can be used as extension functions.

- The shortened forms that you can use to define and call functions make them very suitable to implement DSLs and metaprogramming.

- You cannot have a return in a lambda but you can use a qualified return.

- Lambdas can be simplified to the point where they are difficult to understand. You can use it as a default parameter of a single parameter lambda, leave out parameters using underscore, and execute a lambda immediately.

- All Kotlin functions support closure where variables that were in scope at the time the function was created remain accessible to the function even after they have gone out of scope.

- Inline functions can be used to improve performance and add features such as non-local returns and reification

Chapter 12

Data Classes, Enums & Destructuring

This chapter is about the new features that Kotlin supports to make working with data within a program easier. It isn't about database or file access, which are both largely unchanged from Java. This is about some of the lower level approaches to make representing data within your programs easier and clearer.

Data Classes

If you program in a language other than Java or Kotlin, you may be familiar with structs, structure or records to store data, sometimes along with a few simple methods. In Java and hence Kotlin there are no structs. Instead, to store data, you simply create a class that has the properties corresponding to the data you want to store.

For example:

```
class MyPersonClass{
    var firstName:String=""
    var secondName:String=""
    var age:Int=0
}
```

This is a simple class that can be used to store a person's name and age.

For example:

```
val person1=MyPersonClass()
    person1.firstName="Mickey"
    person1.secondName="Mouse"
    person1.age=89
```

Other languages permit the use of classes in exactly this way, so why do they have structs? The answer is for efficiency. Structs are generally value types, and this can make processing data faster. As long as the overhead of building reference-based objects from classes is low, there is no need to introduce a second entity capable of storing data.

A data class is just a class that does nothing but store data. Kotlin's primary constructor syntax makes it very easy to create a data class as you simply have to list the properties as `val` or `var` in the primary constructor. Thus the previous example can be written:

```
class MyPersonClass(
    var firstName:String="",
    var secondName:String="",
    var age:Int=0
)
```

This is slightly simpler and the class so created is exactly the same, but you can now initialize the properties using the primary constructor:

```
val person1=MyPersonClass(firstName="Mickey",
                          secondName="Mouse",age=89)
```

Notice that you can create private properties by putting `private` in front of the parameter and read-only properties by using `val` in place of `var`.

You can also include the modifier `data` in front of the class definition to create a Kotlin data class. In this case the properties are created as before but the compiler also generates some standard utility methods:

```
data class MyPersonClass(
    var firstName:String="",
    var secondName:String="",
    var age:Int=0
)
```

Now you also have automatically generated methods for:

◆ **equals – used for testing equality of content of two data classes**
The `equals` method is used to implement the == relational operator. This tests for equality of type and content. That is, if two instances of the data object have the same data stored in their properties, == is true. Compare this to the === operator which tests for equality of reference, i.e. do two variables reference the same object?

Equality is such an important topic that it deserves a section to itself, see below

◆ **hashcode – generates a hash code based on the content**
The `hashcode` method computes a unique hash for every object, but for a data class the `hashcode` is only computed using the data properties, which means two instances of the class with the same data have the same hash code.

More on this in the section on Kotlin equality.

- **componentN** – **access functions used in destructuring**

  Basically these are functions that allow other functions to access the data properties without knowing their names. They allow data classes to be used in destructuring – see later. For example:

  ```
  val(firstName,secondName,age)=person1
  ```
  automatically stores each of the properties in the variables on the left.

Notice that assignment is based on property order and not the names involved, see the section on destructuring later in this chapter.

- **toString** – **a function that uses the content to create a string**

  The default `toString` method simply consists of the name of class followed by the hash value of the instance e.g:

  ```
  MyPersonClass@5e2de80c
  ```

The generated `toString` for a data class creates a string with each property and its current value. For example, if you don't put data in front of the class declaration then you still get inherited `equals`, `hashcode` and `toString` methods, but these are inherited from the `Any` class and are very basic – in particular they don't make use of the data proportion. With a data class you get compiler generated custom methods tailored to the data in the class. For example, an instance of the `MyPersonClass` generates:

```
MyPersonClass(firstName=Mickey, secondName=Mouse, age=89)
```

- **copy** – **makes a copy of an instance**

  The copy method will create the new instance for you and set its properties to the same values as the old instance. For example to create a copy of an instance of `MyPersonClass` all you need is:

  ```
  val person3=person1.copy()
  ```

The generated copy method has default values set to the current values of the instance being copied. For example, in the case of the `MyPersonClass`, copy is defined as:

```
fun copy(firstName:String=this.firstName,
        secondName:String=this.secondName,
        var age:Int=this.age)
```

This means that if you want to change any of the properties during the copy you can by providing new values that override the defaults. For example:

```
val person3=person1.copy(firstName="Minnie")
```

changes just the `firstName` property.

This is a technique worth remembering.

Equality

A fundamental task in programming is to work out when two things are equal. This is especially important in the case of data classes, and it is the reason the system generates a custom `equals` method for you.

Kotlin has two equality operators == and === and their negation != and !==.

The simpler operator is === which is a reference equality. This just tests to see if two variables are referencing the same object. For example:

```
val person1=MyPersonClass(firstName="Mickey",
                          secondName="Mouse",age=89)
val person2=MyPersonClass(firstName="Mickey",
                          secondName="Mouse",age=89)
println( person1 === person2 )
```

Prints `false` as even though the data classes may appear to be equal given they have the same property values, they are different objects that just happen to have the same property values.

The == operator tests for structural equality.

That is, all of the objects have to have identical properties. If this is the case then they are considered equal. Notice that the == operator is used in many other comparison operations – `in`, `contains` and so on.

The == operator is implemented by the equals function for the type being compared. If you implement your own classes and you want to compare them then you need to override the `equals` method that you inherit from `Any`.

The Kotlin documentation states that any `equals` method must behave like an equality operator. It should be:

- reflexive, i.e. `a==a` is true
- symmetric, i.e. if `a==b` is true then `b==a`
- transitive, i.e. if `a==b` and `b==c` then `a==c`

It should also be consistent in the sense it should return the same result on repeated testing if there are no changes to the objects involved.

There is another less obvious condition. If two objects are equal then their `hashCode` functions should return the same hash value. What this means is that if you override `equals` you have to override `hashCode` as well.

The big problem with `equals` is that the default implementation inherited from `Any` only compares references. That is by default `equals` and hence === is the same as ==. Many standard classes, and all primitive data types, override `equals` to give you the result you would expect, but not all.

For example, for arrays the `equals` method is still the one inherited from `Any` and hence two arrays are considered equal only if the variables reference the same array object.

This is sometimes what you need, but if you really want to discover if two distinct arrays are equal based on their content then you have to use:

`a contentEquals b`

This is an infix operator which compares elements of each array and returns `true` if they are all equal. This works unless one of the element is itself an array when the elements are compared referentially.

If you want elements that are themselves arrays to be compared structurally you need to use:

`a contentDeepEquals b`

This compares any elements that might be arrays structurally at any level in the structure. Notice that there are deep versions of `hashCode` and `toString`.

Arrays indicate the basic problem with defining equality for general classes. Do you implement a shallow equality that simply compares properties that happen to be objects referentially or do you do a deep compare that compares such objects structurally and so on.

In the case of data classes, `List`, `Map` and `Set`, Kotlin performs a shallow structural comparison. For an array the order of the elements is important. An array with the same values as another but in a different order is not equal. If two maps have the same set of key/value pairs then they are equal irrespective of the order they were added. For two sets to be equal they simply have have the same elements in any order.

The notion of what constitutes equality is a very varied idea. For example is 123 equal to "123"? In most case you need to check any inherited or standard implementation of equals you may have, and see that it fits in with what you mean by equality. You also need to be ready to implement your own `equals` and `hashCode` methods.

Enums

Enums or enumerations are a way of creating ordinal data types.

That is, an ordinal data type is one that is essentially a set of named integer values. For example, a classic use of enum is to represent the days of the week as something that looks like a set of named constants `Monday`, `Tuesday`, `Wednesday`, `Thursday`, `Friday`, `Saturday`, `Sunday` instead of `0,1,2,3,4,5,6`. Behind the scenes of an enum there are a set of integers which identify the particular constant and provide an order relation. That is `Monday<Tuesday` because `0<1`. The integer associated with an enum is generally called its ordinal or ordinal position.

In both Java and Kotlin, but not in many other languages, the enum data type is a class and this provides lots of additional features and possibilities. You declare an enum class by putting the enum modifier in front of a fairly standard class declaration:

```
enum class Days{Monday, Tuesday, Wednesday, Thursday,
                          Friday, Saturday, Sunday}
```

Notice that the enumeration of names is presented as if it was the body of the class being defined and in a sense it is. Each of the names is converted into a property of the Days enum class which in turn behaves like a static class and a type.

For example to declare a variable suitable for holding values from the enumeration you would use:

```
var myDay:Days
```

and to store a value in myDay:

```
myDay=Days.Monday
```

You can use an enum in conditionals and when statements to make your code more readable. For example:

```
var myDay:Days=Days.Monday
if(myDay==Days.Monday)
```

If myDay is of type Days what type is Days.Monday?

The answer is that it is of type Days as well. The peculiar thing about an enum is that it is a static class that has properties that are instances of the same type. This observation is the key to understanding, and getting the most out, of enums.

The instances of the enum come with few standard methods, the most important of which are name and ordinal. As you can guess, name returns the string that is the name of the instance, and ordinal, an integer indicating its position in the enumeration sequence.

Notice that there is only one instance of each of the enum classes and this is shared between all of the variables that make use of it. That is:

```
var myDay=Days.Monday
```

and:

```
var yourDay=Days.Monday
```

both reference the same instance of Days i.e. Days.Monday. This can be important to know if you extend the enum class.

As Kotlin allows an enum class to be declared with properties and methods just like any other class, you can now see that you can extend what an enum can do.

For example, we can add a method to each of the days of the week to indicate if it is working or non-working. However, we have a small syntax problem. How do you indicate when the list of enum properties has ended and the rest of the class declaration starts? The Kotlin answer is that you use a single semicolon to mark the two sections:

```
enum class Days {Monday, Tuesday, Wednesday, Thursday,
                        Friday, Saturday, Sunday
;
    fun isWorking() {
        if (this.name == "Saturday" || this.name == "Sunday") {
            println("non-working")
        } else {
            println("working")
        }
    }
}
```

With this definition each of the enum properties has a new method isWorking:

```
var myDay: Days = Days.Saturday
myDay.isWorking()
```

which prints non-working.

Notice that this method is an instance method and not part of the static myDays object. This, however, does have some predefined methods:

   ◆   **values** – returns an array of all of the enum values

For example:

```
println(Days.values()[1].name)
```

displays "Tuesday".

   ◆   **valuesOf(string)** - returns the enum object that has a name that exactly matches the string

For example:

```
println(Days.valueOf("Monday").ordinal)
```

prints 0.

Not only can you add methods and properties to each instance, you can also define a constructor.

For example if we add a primary constructor to Days we can add a workingHours property that each of the instances initialize:

```
enum class Days(val workingHours:Int) {
    Monday(10), Tuesday(10), Wednesday(5), Thursday(10),
                Friday(5), Saturday(0), Sunday(0)
}
```

Now each enum instance has a workingHours property:

```
println(myDay.workingHours)
```

It is occasionally useful to see other ways of doing things and so here is a secondary constructor approach to implementing workingHours:

```
enum class Days {
    Monday(10), Tuesday(10), Wednesday(5), Thursday(10),
                        Friday(5), Saturday(0), Sunday(0)
    ;
    val workingHours: Int
    constructor(workingHours: Int) {
        this.workingHours = workingHours
    }
}
```

Perhaps the ultimate customization of each of the enum instances is to define each one using an anonymous class. This allows each one to have its own implementation of abstract methods.

For example we could implement workingHours as a custom function defined for each enum:

```
enum class Days {
    Monday {
        override fun workingHours() = 10
    },
    Tuesday {
        override fun workingHours() = 10
    },
    Wednesday {
        override fun workingHours() = 5
    },
    Thursday {
        override fun workingHours() = 10
    },
    Friday {
        override fun workingHours() = 5
    },
    Saturday {
        override fun workingHours() = 0
    },
    Sunday {
        override fun workingHours() = 0
    }
    ;
    abstract fun workingHours(): Int
}
```

Now of course we have to call `workingHours` as a function:

```
println(myDay.workingHours())
```

Notice that the importance of this simple example is that in principle each of the overridden functions could do its job in an entirely different way. Perhaps Friday could generate a random number for `workingHours`.

Sealed Classes – A Better Enum?

An enum is a set of classes associated with an ordinal, but each ordinal has only one instance of the class. Sealed classes are an attempt to be more flexible but they lack the convenience of enums – you have to do more of the work.

To show how they compare let's use a sealed class to implement the days of the week enumeration:

```
sealed class Days {
    class Monday : Days()
    class Tuesday : Days()
    class Wednesday ; Days()
    class Thursday:Days()
    class Friday:Days()
    class Saturday:Days()
    class Sunday:Days()
}
```

With this definition you can use the enumeration in almost the same way, but `Days` is now a class and there are no static properties corresponding to the enum instances.

You can set a variable to a value of the class using:

```
var myDays: Days = Days.Wednesday()
```

just like an `enum`, but `Days` is a type not an object so to test for a value you have to use:

```
if(myDays is Days.Wednesday) println("it is wed")
```

One of the advantages of using a sealed class is that if you use a `when` expression the compiler will check that you have included all of the possible value. This is what the sealed modifier does for you. It tells the compiler that the sealed class only has the distinct list of subtypes and no more. This allows the compilor to check that you have created a `when` expression that doesn't miss any of them.

Notice that this only works for a when expression, i.e. one that returns a value, and not for a when statement that doesn't.

For example:
```
fun test(myDays: Days):String {
    return when (myDays) {
        is Days.Monday ->"Its monday"
        is Days.Tuesday -> "its tuesday"
        is Days.Wednesday -> "its wedensday"
        is Days.Thursday -> "its thursday"
        is Days.Friday -> "its friday"
        is Days.Saturday -> "its saturday"
        is Days.Sunday -> "its sunday"
    }
}
```

In this case if you leave one of the days out the compiler will flag an error. Normally you have to have an else clause in a when to make it complete.

This is all the sealed modifier does for you. If you change sealed to open and add an else clause to the when then everything works the same. This is quite a small advantage and while using classes is more flexible you have to do more of the work.

You can also define the classes that derive from a sealed class outside of the sealed class:
```
sealed class Days
class Monday:Days()
class Tuesday:Days()
class Wednesday:Days()
class Thursday:Days()
class Friday:Days()
class Saturday:Days()
class Sunday:Days()
```

In this case you can refer to the derived classes directly without needing to mention the sealed class itself:
```
var myDays: Days = Wednesday()
if(myDays is Wednesday) println("it is wed")
```

This might lead to a more readable code but it also makes name clashes possible. All of the derived classes of a sealed class have to be defined in the same file.

If you want to add a name and ordinal property you can:
```
sealed class Days(val name:String,val ordinal:Int)
class Monday : Days("Monday",0)
class Tuesday : Days("Tuesday",1)
class Wednesday : Days("Wednesday",2)
class Thursday:Days("Thursday",3)
class Friday:Days("Friday",4)
class Saturday:Days("Saturday",5)
class Sunday:Days("Sunday",6)
```

and now you create a day using the same code but you can access name and ordinal properties:

```
var myDays: Days = Wednesday()
println(myDays.name)
```

The advantage of using a class is that now you aren't restricted to a single instance for a particular day. For example you can add a working hours property:

```
class Wednesday(var workingHours:Int=0):Days("Wednesday",2)
```

The other days of the week would be defined in the same way. Now we can create two Wednesdays with different working hours:

```
var myDay1=Wednesday(10)
var myDay2=Wednesday(4)
println(myDay1.workingHours)
println(myDay2.workingHours)
```

and you get 10 and 4 printed. If you were using an enum, the instance that represented Wednesday could only hold a single value for workingHours. If you don't need state information of this sort then you can use objects rather than classes within sealed classes.

We could continue to explore this approach and do all sorts of clever things, but it is essentially the application of general object-oriented programming techniques and not something additional that Kotlin provides.

Delegated Properties

Properties are the way data is represented in an object-oriented language. Each class has the responsibility for creating get and set functions to allow the outside world to modify and access the data. Some types of property are more sophisticated than a simple set and get with backing variables.

For example, a property might keep a history of its previous values or it might call registered callbacks when its value changes – observable properties and so on. You can implement these mechanisms on a class-by-class basis but this isn't particularly efficient, and if you want to change the way a property works you will have to go round all of the classes and change them all.

Kotlin provides a way to delegate property implementation to another class. It also allows you to delegate a local variable in a function which isn't a property in the same way:

For example to delegate a property:

```
class myClass {
 var myProperty:Int by myDelegate()
}
```

and to delegate a local variable:

```
fun mFunction(){
        var myLocalVar:Int by myDelegate()
        println(myLocalVar)
    }
```

In this case the delegate is an instance of the class myDelegate. This has to provide a get and set function with a particular signature. The get is:

```
operator fun getValue(thisRef:Any?,property:KProperty<*>):T
```

and the set is:

```
operator fun setValue(thisRef:Any?,property:KProperty<*>,value:T)
```

where thisRef is the object doing the delegating, property is an object that represents the property, value is the value to be set and T is the type of the property. Notice that for a local variable Any will be set to null as there is no object doing the delegating. We also need to add:

```
import kotlin.reflect.KProperty
```

to use Kproperty.

So in the case of our myClass example with an Int parameter, myDelegate might be:

```
class myDelegate{
 operator fun getValue(thisRef:Any?, property:KProperty<*>):Int{
    return 1
 }
 operator fun setValue(thisRef:Any?,property:KProperty<*>,value:Int)
 {
 }
}
```

where for simplicity of the example, the get returns 1 and the set throws the value away.

If you want to make sure the get and set are correct or want the system to generate stubs simply implement one of the standard interfaces ReadOnlyProperty<R,T> or ReadyWriteProperty<R,T> where R is the type of thisRef and T is the type of the property.

If we try to use the property just defined:

```
val myObject=myClass()
println(myObject.myProperty)
```

You will see 1 printed. Notice that the system has created an instance of `myDelegate` to use with `myObject`. Every time you create an instance of `myObject` you get a new instance of `myDelegate` to work with it.

For example, if we change the delegate so that a backing property is used to implement the functioning of a standard property:

```
class myDelegate{
  private var backing:Int=0
  operator fun getValue(thisRef:Any, property:KProperty<*>):Int{
    return backing
  }
  operator fun setValue(thisRef:Any,property:KProperty<*>,value:Int)
  {
    backing=value
  ]
}
```

then you can see that each instance of `myClass` gets it own instance of `myDelegate`:

```
val myObject1=myClass()
val myObject2=myClass()
myObject1.myProperty=1
myObject2.myProperty=2
println(myObject1.myProperty)
println(myObject2.myProperty)
```

The final print statements print 1 and 2 respectively, showing that the instances don't share the property.

You can pass data including lambdas.

One of the best examples of delegation is the `Observable` which is one of the three standard delegated properties that Kotlin provides – `Lazy` and `Map` being the other two.

The `observable` delegate accepts two parameters. The first is the initial value of the delegated property and the second is a function to be executed whenever the property changes. This function has the signature `prop, old, new` which give the property being changed, and its old and new values.

For example:

```
class myClass {
    var name: String by Delegates.observable("<no name>") {
        prop, old, new -> println(new)
    }
}
```

To make this work you have to import the `Delegates` package:

```
import kotlin.properties.Delegates
```

The delegated property is used in the same way as any other, but with the side effect that it prints the new value:

```
val myObject=myClass()
myObject.name="Mickey"
myObject.name="Minnie"
```

You will see `Mickey` and `Minnie` printed.

Taking the customization of the delegate object even further you can define your own `provideDelegate` operator. When you create an instance of a class that uses a delegate property then the system automatically creates an instance of the delegate class for you. If you need to, you can do the job yourself by defining the `provideDelegate` operator as a member or extension function of the delegate class. The `provideDelegate` is called to create the instance of the delegate class. It receives the same parameters as the `get` function i.e. `thisRef` and `property`, and it has to return an instance of the delegate.

For example to add the `provideDelegate` operator to our trivial example from earlier:

```
class myDelegate {
    operator fun provideDelegate(thisRef: MyClass,
                                 prop: KProperty<*>): myDelegate {
        println("creating delegate")
        return myDelegate()
    }
    private var backing: Int = 0
    operator fun getValue(thisRef: Any,
                          property: KProperty<*>): Int {
        return backing
    }
    operator fun setValue(thisRef: Any,
                    property: KProperty<*>, value: Int) {
        backing = value
    }
}
```

Now when we create an instance you will see "creating delegate" printed:

```
class MyClass {
    var myProperty: Int by myDelegate()
}

fun main(args: Array<String>) {
    val myObject = MyClass()
    myObject.myProperty = 1
    println(myObject.myProperty)
}
```

Of course, in practice the `provideDelegate` operator can do whatever it needs to check the validity of the delegation and to build a custom object to do the job.

You don't need to know how delegate properties work, but it isn't complicated. When you declare a delegate property the system creates a hidden property with the name `propertyname$delegate`, which is a reference to an instance of the delegate class `this`:

```
private val propertyname$delegate=MyDelegate()
```

The generated `get` and `set` for the property simply hands off to the instance of the delegate class, e.g:

```
get()=propertyname$delegate.getValue(this,this::propertyname)
set(value:type)=propertyname$delegate.getValue(this,
                                        this::propertyname,value)
```

Once you have seen a delegate property in action you should be able to generalize and take the idea in whatever direction you need it to go.

Destructuring

Destructuring is a sophisticated sounding name for a very simple idea. Sometimes you have a data structure with a number of elements or properties and you want to unpack these into a set of standalone variables.

For example, if we have a data class:

```
data class MyDataClass(var name:String,var age:Int)
```

Then we can create an instance and use destructuring to pack the data into separate variables:

```
var myDataObject=MyDataClass("Mickey",89)
var (myName,myAge) = myDataObject
println(myName)
println(myAge)
```

The destructuring assignment:

```
var (myName,myAge) = myDataObject
```

is converted into:

```
var myName = myDataObject.component1()
var myAge = myDataObject.component2()
```

For a data object the operator methods `component1`, `component2` and so on are automatically generated. This is the reason why if you take the `data` modifier from the start of the declaration you will get an error message as the class no longer has `componentN` methods.

Of course, you can add them manually:

```
class MyDataClass(var name:String,var age:Int){
    operator fun component1()=name
    operator fun component2()=age
}
```

In fact any class that has `componentN` operator methods can be used in a destructuring operation.

As well as assignment destructuring can be used in `for` loops.

For example:

```
val myList=listOf(MyDataClass("Mickey",89),MyDataClass("Minnie",88))
    for ((name,age) in myList){
        println(name)
        println(age)
    }
```

As long as each element that the iterator returns supports destructuring, you can use this sort of `for` loop.

Destructuring can also allow a function to seem to return multiple values.

For example:

```
fun myFavouriteMouse():MyDataClass{
    return MyDataClass("Mickey",89)
 }
```

and you can now write:

```
var (myName,myAge)=myFavouriteMouse()
```

which looks as if `myFavouriteMouse` returns multiple values in the same way that you can in Python.

If you don't want to make use of a destructure value you can use an underscore to leave it out:

```
var (_,myAge)=myFavouriteMouse()
```

Finally, you can use destructuring in parameters of lambdas as long as the parameter type has `componentN` operator functions. Notice that this makes adding an extra set of parenthesis in a lambda an error. That is:

```
{ a,b-> statements that use a and b}
{(a,b)-> statements that use a and b}
```

are different in that the second one accepts a single parameter that can be destructured to give a and b.

For example:

```
val myLambda= {(name,age):MyDataClass->
      println(name)
      println(age)
   }
```

This looks like a lambda that would accept two parameters, but because of destructuring it accepts a single instance of MyDataClass:

```
val myDataObject=MyDataClass("Mickey",89)
myLambda(myDataObject)
```

This works with any class that supports componentN operator methods.

The Spread Operator

There is one special type of destructuring designed to make it easier to use varargs. If you pass parameters to a vararg one by one it builds an array for you to hold them.

What if you already have the arguments in an array?

This is where the spread operator * comes in. It allows you to pass an array directly to the varargs as an array. You can think of it as unpacking the array into separate parameters which is why it can be regarded as a destructuring operator.

For example:

```
val a=arrayOf(1,2,3)
val list =asList(*a)
```

The asList method expects a vararg of the individual elements that will be used to create the list. The spread operator passes the array as if it was a set of individual parameters.

Summary

- Kotlin doesn't provide structs or any value alternative to classes, but it does provide a data class which has data properties and a set of methods to work with them.

- Equality is a difficult thing to define in an object-oriented world. There are two basic equality operators == for equality of reference and === for structural or content equality.

- If you want equality to be correctly interpreted for your custom classes you need to implement your own `equals` method. This can either perform a shallow or a deep comparison.

- Arrays have a referential definition of equals, but you can also use `contentEquals` for a shallow structural equals and `contentDeepEquals` for a deep structural equals.

- Data classes, `List`, `Map` and `Set` have a generated shallow equals.

- Enums allow you to construct ordinal data representations that map names to integers. An `enum` behaves like a static class that has properties that are instances of the same type.

- An `enum` can have properties and methods but these are shared between all instances of the type.

- Sealed classes provide an alternative to enum but you have to do more work to implement similar behavior. They work like a set of derived classes that form a known set. The compiler will check that you have included them all in a `when` expression.

- Delegation is an alternative to inheritance and you can automatically delegate property implementation to a specific object that implements a delegated interface.

- Destructuring is a simple mechanism for unpacking the data contained in a structure into individual variables.

- The spread operator * allows you to pass an array to a `vararg` parameter.

Chapter 13

Exceptions, Annotations & Reflection

In this chapter we look at three loosely connected topics. Annotation and reflection work together to allow you to bring metaprogramming to Kotlin. Exceptions are a way of dealing with "out of band" behavior and could almost be considered to be part of metaprogramming. All three qualify for the status of something that you tackle when you have become completely comfortable with the main features of Kotlin.

Exceptions

Exceptions in Kotlin work in the way that they do in most modern languages, and of course Java. There are some interesting differences, however.

An exception is an error or a fault condition that is difficult to test for before it happens, but it has to be admitted that many exceptions are simply excuses not to test for the error.
For example, division by zero is an error that can usually be tested for beforehand:

```
if(b!=0) result=a/b
```

but in most cases it is treated an exception to the normal flow of control within the program.

The whole idea of exception handling is that it can provide a sort of alternative flow of control for your code so that you can express your algorithm in two clear parts – one for what happens when everything works, and another for what happens when there is a problem.

Exceptions also allow you to unwind the call stack to get back to an earlier condition that represents things before the error occurred so that you can have another attempt.

In Kotlin and Java exceptions are handled using a try-catch block:

```
try{
    var result=a/b
}
catch(e:ArithmeticException){
    println(e)
}
```

The statements within the try block are executed and control passes out of the try-catch to the next instruction if everything works.

If there is a problem while the program is running, then an exception is thrown and the catch blocks are checked in the order they occur for one that matches the type of the exception object. Exceptions "throw" an exception object and all exception objects are descended from Throwable.

Which exception a catch block handles is determined by the type of the catch parameter. If the exception object is of that type or a subtype then the catch block is executed and the program continues after the try-catch block.

There can be multiple catch blocks after a try and each one can handle a different possible exception. In this way the catch blocks form a multi-way selection, with the same form as a when, for what is to happen based on the type of the thrown object.

Notice that unlike Java, Kotlin doesn't currently support multi-catch expressions. That is, you can't use a single catch to handle more than one type of exception if they are not derived classes.

If the exception is unhandled, i.e. there is no catch block, then a return is executed and the next function up the call stack is checked for an exception handler that accepts the exception. If one is not found a return is executed and the search for an exception handler continues. Eventually the top level is reached and if no exception handler is found the program halts with a run-time exception which is reported to the user. This unwinding of the call stack is the reason that an exception can get back to an early part of the program that can try the task again or give better error information to the user.

For example, if we define a function to do the division:

```
fun div(a:Int,b:Int):Int=a/b
```

and call it from within a try-catch block:

```
try{
    div(1,0)
}
catch(e:ArithmeticException){
    println(e)
}
```

Then the exception occurs in the div function, but because it is unhandled it is passed up to the main program which does handle it.

You can also add a finally block at the end, and this contains code that will always be executed no matter what happens. The finally block is an important facility because it can be used to remove resources that might have been created. The classic example is to use a finally block to close all the files that might have been opened.

Notice that a `finally` block is called whether or not an exception has occurred. As a result it is sometimes useful to have a `try` block with a `finally` and no `catch` blocks.

For example:

```
try{
 do lots of things
}
finally{
 clean up after doing lots of things
}
```

A `finally` block will be executed, even if the `try` block contains a `return` that ends the function.

One big difference between Java and Kotlin is that the `try` block is actually an expression. Its value is the last expression in the `try` or the `catch` that is executed. It is also worth pointing out that the `try` block is a nested block and hence any variables you might declare within it are local to that block.

So for example:

```
try{
    var result=a/b
}
```

in this case `result` isn't available outside of the `try` block. However, as `try` is an expression:

```
var result=try{
                a/b
            }
        catch(e:ArithmeticException){
            0
            }
```

you can access the result of the division in the main program and the result is zero if an exception occurs. If the `try` or `catch` block doesn't return a value then the expression evaluates to `Unit`.

Another big difference between Kotlin and Java exceptions is that Kotlin doesn't have checked exceptions. Put simply, a checked exception is one that you have to handle and the compiler does a compile-time check to make sure you have. This seemed like a good idea when it was first introduced into Java, but it resulted a great many `catch` clauses that didn't do anything - either because there was no time to create something meaningful or the programmer knew that an exception of the type was logically impossible.

You can argue about the usefulness of checked exceptions, but Kotlin doesn't have them.

You can create your own exceptions by creating a subclass of `Throwable` or one of the existing exception classes. To throw an exception all you have to do is create an instance of the exception class and use it in a `throw` statement:

```
throw myException()
```

You can throw an exception from within an exception handler, i.e. a `try` or `catch` block, and this is a common way of passing exceptions to other handlers.

Just as `try` is an expression, so is `throw`, but it returns the `Nothing` type. Of course, a `throw` doesn't allow execution to continue, so it might seem strange to have a value at all. The only point of `throw` returning `Nothing` is that it allows it to be included in expressions, i.e. the compiler doesn't complain if you write things like:

```
val myVal=myObject.name ?: throw myException()
```

This either assigns `myVal` a non null value, or it throws an exception and stops the evaluation.

The big problem with exception handling is the cost of implementing anything that works reasonably well from the user's point of view. Every task within a program should be protected by an exception handler that attempts to recover the situation. This can increase the amount of code needed by a factor of at least ten. While it is difficult to write a program that works when everything goes according to plan, it is next to impossible to write one that still works when things start to go wrong.

Exceptions are a good idea, rarely used sufficiently.

Annotations

Annotations are a strange idea when you first meet them.

At their simplest you can regard them as instructions to the compiler.

For example. you can change the name of the default class used to host functions that are not explicitly declared as methods using an annotation:

```
@file:JvmName("class name")
```

This is an instruction to the compiler to change the name and you cannot hope to implement custom annotations with a similar power unless you are prepared to modify the compiler.

There are a few standard annotations and you can create your own custom annotations, although as indicated these don't integrate with the compiler in quite the same way.

Custom annotations are generally used to pass information either to another programmer or to the code itself.

For example the @Deprecated annotation marks a function as being one to avoid using because it is going to be removed in the future:

```
@Deprecated("Do not Use")
fun div(a:Int,b:Int):Int=a/b
```

If you try to use the deprecated function then the compiler will show that there is a problem by showing it in struck out and display a suitable message:

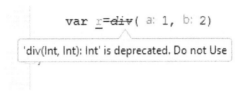

In this case you can see that the annotation is of use to any programmer building a library for others to use. It communicates information about how the function should be used to other programmers. Some annotations also indicate conditions to code that makes use of it, but to follow how this works we need to know about reflection and so this topic is deferred until later in the chapter.

Annotations can be applied to classes, functions, properties and so on.

There is a particular problem with using annotations in Kotlin because of the need to remain compatible with Java annotations. The problem is that Kotlin doesn't always expose all of the equivalent Java elements that an annotation may be applied to, and you may well want to annotate these "hidden" elements.

To get around this problem, Kotlin has some rules for writing annotations:

To apply an annotation to a primary constructor you have to use the constructor keyword in the declaration:

```
class MyClass @Deprecated("Do not use") constructor(val MyProp:Int)
```

You can annotate a lambda by writing the annotation in front of the opening curly bracket:

```
@Deprecated("Do not use") {rest of lambda}
```

To attach an Annotation to a Java entity you have to specify the entity before writing the annotation.

The supported entities are:

- ◆ `file`
- ◆ `property` (annotations with this target are not visible to Java)
- ◆ `field`
- ◆ `get` (property getter)
- ◆ `set` (property setter)
- ◆ `receiver` (receiver parameter of an extension function or property)
- ◆ `param` (constructor parameter)
- ◆ `setparam` (property setter parameter)
- ◆ `delegate` (the field storing the delegate instance for a delegated property)

So, for example, to annotate the setter of a Kotlin property you would use:

```
class MyClass{
 @set:Deprecated("Do Not Use")
 var myProp
}
```

You can also set multiple annotations on an entity by following the entity name by a list of annotations in square brackets.

Annotations are useful when you want to associate data, usually referred to as metadata, to your code. To do this you have to create custom annotation classes and to make use of them you have to resort to reflection.

So first we need to look at reflection and then return to custom annotations.

Reflection

Reflection is an advanced technique that gives you access to things that you don't normally have access to. To make use of it you have to import classes from `kotlin.reflection`.

You can use it to find out details of the classes and their methods and properties – things that you might suppose would not be accessible at run time. As you might expect, Kotlin's reflection features are somewhat different to Java's, but as always there are ways of working with Java reflection.

The most basic form of reflection is to get an object, an instance of `KClass`, that corresponds to a Kotlin class.

To retrieve the `class` as a `KClass` object all you have to do is:

```
val classobj=MyClass::class
```

What you do next is to access any of the class details you care to, using the methods and properties of the classobj.

For example suppose MyClass is:

```
class MyClass{
    fun myMethod1(){}
    fun myMethod2(){}
}
```

Then you can discover what member functions the class has using:

```
val classobj=MyClass::class
for(m in classobj.declaredMemberFunctions){
 println(m.name)
}
```

This lists the methods by name. Methods and functions in general are represented by KCallable objects.

You can do some things you might not expect to be able to do in a statically-typed language like Kotlin (or Java).

For example, once you have the KClass object you can create an instance:

```
var myObject=classobj.createInstance()
```

and you can call methods on that instance:

```
myObject.myMethod1()
```

You can even call a method that you have obtained by reflection. The only thing you need to remember is that you have to supply the parameters correctly and the first parameter is this, i.e. the call context or receiver.

For example:

```
for(m in classobj.declaredMemberFunctions){
        println(m.name)
        m.call(myObject)
    }
```

The this that you pass has to be the correct type of object.

You can also get a KClass object from an instance of the class:

```
val c=myObject::class
```

Properties can also be manipulated and in this case the objects you need to look up are the KProperty and KMutableProperty classes.

We have already seen the use of the :: operator to get a reference to a function. It can also be used to get a reference to a bound method.

For example:

```
val myFunction=::myObject.myMethod
```

stores a reference to myMethod bound to myObject. Now when you call myFunction() it calls myMethod with this set to myObject.

You can also gain access to the Java reflection methods using the Kotlin `KClass java` property.

When you first meet reflection it seems to give you great power, but with great power come great bugs.

Use reflection sparingly if at all. Most of the difficulty is finding the method or property of the reflection classes that provides what you need. It may be obvious, but it is worth saying that you cannot use reflection to change the definition of a class. You cannot add methods or properties at run time. You can only inquire about, and make use of, members that were added at compile time.

Custom Annotations

Now that we have covered some aspects of reflection we can deal more easily with custom annotations.

It is very easy to create a custom annotation. All you need to is create a class with the modifier `annotation`:

```
annotation class MyAnnotation
```

Now you have an annotation ready to use:

```
@MyAnnotation class MyClass{...}
```

All you can really do with such a simple annotation class is to check to see if some entity has the annotation at run time using reflection.

For example, the `KClass` object has an `annotations` property that returns a list of annotations:

```
val myClassObject = MyClass::class
  for (a in myClassObject.annotations) {
      println(a.annotationClass.simpleName)
  }
```

This just prints `MyAnnotation`.

The only complication is that an annotation can be attached to a class or any member of a class/object. You have to use reflection to retrieve an object that represents that entity, and then use annotations to retrieve its annotations.

If you just want to check that a single type of annotation has been applied then you can use `findAnnotation` which returns any annotation object of the specified type or null if none exist:

```
val myAnnotationObject=myClassObject.findAnnotation<MyAnnotation>()
```

Notice that as a nullable type you have to continue to check for null in the returned value, e.g.:

```
println(myAnnotationObject?.annotationClass?.simpleName)
```

As well as simple bare annotations you can also include some data as
Annotation classes can have a primary constructor.

For example, you might want to record the name of the programmer who
created the entity:

```
annotation class MyAnnotation(val programmerName:String="Unknown")
```

By providing a default value, the user of the annotation doesn't have to
supply the information but they can override it:

```
@MyAnnotation("Mike") class MyClass {...}
```

You can retrieve the data as a property of the annotation class retrieved by
either annotations or findAnnotation:

```
val myAnnotationObject=myClassObject.findAnnotation<MyAnnotation>()
println(myAnnotationObject?.programmerName)
```

There are also a range of annotations that you can apply to custom
annotations:

- @Target specifies the possible kinds of elements which can be
  annotated with the annotation (classes, functions, properties,
  expressions etc.);

- @Retention specifies whether the annotation is stored in the compiled
  class files and whether it's visible through reflection at run time (by
  default, both are true);

- @Repeatable allows using the same annotation on a single element
  multiple times;

- @MustBeDocumented specifies that the annotation is part of the public
  API and should be included in the class or method signature shown in
  the generated API documentation.

The one you are likely to use most often is @Target to restrict the range of
entities that the annotation can be applied to. For example:

```
@Target(AnnotationTarget.CLASS)
annotation class MyAnnotation(val programmerName:String="Unknown")
```

sets MyAnnotation as usable only on classes. If you try to use it on something
other than a class you generate a compiler error message:

```
26        @MyAnnotation("Mike") fun myFunction(){}
```

This annotation is not applicable to target 'local function'

You can include multiple targets in the @Target annotation.

Annotations can include annotations as properties set in their primary constructors and things can become complicated. Kotlin annotations also work with Java annotations.

In general, you need to think carefully about using annotations. They work well where you need to attach information to classes that isn't going to change at the instance level.

You also need to think about the two parts that make an annotation work. There is the annotation class itself, which the programmer uses to attach data to the classes, and other entities they create. Then there is the processing machinery that consumes the annotations. This machinery is usually part of a framework that the user is allowed to extend by adding classes which have to declare their characteristics to the existing classes. This is generally a big undertaking.

In short, custom annotations are not a facility that every project needs to undertake.

Summary

- An exception is an error or a fault condition that is difficult to test for before it happens.

- Exceptions allow you to unwind the call stack to get back to an earlier condition that represents things before the error occurred so that you can have another attempt.

- In Kotlin exceptions are handled using a `try catch` block:
    try{*instructions*}catch(*exception*){handler}

- You can also add a `finally` block at the end, and this contains code that will always be executed no matter what happen.

- The `try` block is an expression that returns the value of the last expression in the `try` or `catch`.

- There are no checked exceptions in Kotlin

- You can throw your own exceptions using the `throw` command.

- Annotations are often used as instructions to the compiler.

- Custom annotations are generally used to pass information either to another programmer or to the code itself.

- Kotlin has some rules for writing annotations that attach to entities that are really only visible in Java.

- Reflection is an advanced technique that gives you access to things that you don't normally have access to at run time like class and methods.

- You can also gain access to the Java reflection methods using the Kotlin `KClass java` property.

- All you need to create custom annotations is a class with the modifier `annotation`

- To work with annotations at run time you have to use reflection to retrieve an object which represents that entity, and then use its annotations property to retrieve its annotations as an array.

- There are a number of annotations which can be applied to a custom annotation to control how it is used.

Chapter 14

Working With Java

This chapter is about how Kotlin can make use of existing Java code.

Using Swing

In this chapter we are going to concentrate on using Java code from Kotlin rather than the other way round. The reason for this orientation is simply that there is a lot of existing Java code out there, and Kotlin generally has to make use of it in the form of precompiled libraries. The situation of needing to use Kotlin code from Java is much less common and, at the moment, is usually a design choice.

On the other hand, the need to use existing Java code is almost essential to any use of Kotlin. For example, you can opt to create complete Android applications by writing nothing but Kotlin, but as the Android libraries are all written in Java you have no choice but to discover how to work with Java objects and their methods and properties. Even a 100% Kotlin Android program has to interact with the system's Java.

If you are starting a new Kotlin project in a general environment then you are going to need to use Java libraries such as Swing or JavaFX to build your user interface. At the moment pure Kotlin programs that target the JVM and make no use of Java code are are rare.

The good news is that Kotlin compiles to byte code that is compatible with Java 6 (you can opt for later versions of Java). What this means is that all of Kotlin's advanced syntax is mostly that – syntax which disappears when compiled. It is because Kotlin uses the same byte code and the same overall structures and libraries that makes it possible for it to claim 100% Java compatibility.

For this reason you can start out with the optimistic view that if you want to use an existing Java library you can. The only problems you might have is finding the right Kotlin syntax to make the correct connection with the Java code. Most of the time it is simply a matter of not using some new feature that Kotlin has introduced or finding out how the new feature maps onto something that exists in Java.

In this chapter we are going to use the Swing GUI library as an example of using Java code. The main reason is that Kotlin doesn't have a GUI library of its own, and while there are newer Java GUI libraries, Swing is still worth using.

If you want to know more about using Android Java code in Kotlin see: **_Android Programming In Kotlin: Starting with an App_** ISBN: 978-1871962543.

Using Java Classes

The most important thing to realize is that Java and Kotlin use the same class implementation at run time – because they both use the JVM which supports classes and objects at a fairly high level. You can import any Java class and create instances using Kotlin syntax, i.e. no need for new.

For example, to create an instance of the Swing JFrame class all you have to write is:

```
val myFrame=JFrame("Hello Word")
```

You also need to include:

```
import javax.swing.*
```

at the start of the file.

If you actually want to see the JFrame then you need to set its size and set it to visible:

```
myFrame.setSize(300,200)
myFrame.setVisible(true)
```

If you run the final program:

```
import javax.swing.*
fun main(args: Array<String>) {
    val myFrame=JFrame("Hello World")
    myFrame.setSize(300,200)
    myFrame.setVisible(true)
}
```

You will see a JFrame open with the title Hello World:

Notice that creating Swing objects on the main program thread isn't the best way to work, but it is a simple way to get started. See how to do it properly in a later section.

Getters & Setters

If the Java method follows the convention for `get` and `set` properties then you can simply use them as if they were Kotlin properties. Note, however, that this only works for methods starting with `get` and no parameters, or starting with `set` and a single parameter.

Interestingly Kotlin can also deal with Booleans that are named starting with `is` and the setter starts with `set` as properties.

So, in our previous example, we can't treat `setSize` as a property because it takes two parameters, but we can treat `isVisible` as a property as it is Boolean with a name starting with `is`:

```
myFrame.isVisible=true
```

You can use the Java `get` and `set` functions but notice that IntelliJ will list all of the properties that it has converted from Java `get` and `set` functions. So if you can't find `setTitle` in the dropdown autocomplete list, look for a `Title` property:

```
myFrame.Title="New Title"
```

is the same as:

```
myFrame.setTitle("New Title")
```

If you are familiar with the Java classes you are using you will sometimes find this confusing.

The Event Dispatch Thread

Now we have to tackle one of the most confusing parts of using Swing, or any GUI framework.

In the previous example we created the `JFrame` using the main thread i.e. the thread of execution that is used to run the `main` function. This is not a good idea. The reason is that when you use Swing another thread is automatically created and this handles all of the events that can be generated by buttons and other components.

This thread is the Event Dispatch Thread or EDT and if you create your JFrame using the main thread, then potentially two different threads will try to interact with it. This might work for a while, but Swing is not thread-safe and sooner or later something strange will happen as two different threads compete to update the UI.

The correct way to work with Swing components is to use the EDT to create and manipulate all of them. The main thread, or any other thread, should never try to access a Swing component.

So how do you run code on the EDT?

This is fairly easy. There are utility functions in SwingUtilities that will take any code you pass to it and run it on the EDT. The exact mechanism is that the code is added to the event queue, and after all the events that were ahead of it have been processed the EDT will run it.

There are two utility functions that will run code on the EDT - `invokeLater` which adds the code to the event queue and returns immediately and `invokeAndWait` which adds the code to the event queue and doesn't return until the code has completed. Both accept a `Runnable` and this is particularly easy to arrange in Kotlin, but first we need to look at how lambdas are converted into SAMs.

SAM Conversions

A SAM is a class or Interface with a Single Abstract Method. They are what Java often uses to allow you to create something that looks like a function. When a function is needed all you do is create an instance of the SAM that represents it and implement the method that stands in for the function.

For example, Java has the `Runnable` interface with the single abstract method `run`. This is the method that you implement to define code that should be executed on a different thread. That is, you implement `Runnable` and the `run` method and then use:

```
Thread t=new Thread(myRunnable)
t.start()
```

to execute the code you created in the `run` method on a new thread.

This isn't difficult once you understand it, but having to create an instance of a class just to pass a function to another function is verbose and it is what lambdas were invented to make easier.

The Kotlin compiler will automatically recognize when you are passing a lambda as a parameter to a method that requires a SAM, defined as an Interface, to be passed and will convert the lambda to a SAM.

That is, it takes the code in your lambda and wraps it in an instance of the SAM automatically without you having to do anything.

For example you can write the previous use of `Runnable` as:

```
val t=Thread({System.out.println("Hello New Thread")})
t.start()
```

Notice that the parameter is a lambda in curly brackets. Using the rule that a final lambda parameter can be passed outside of the function's parentheses we can write this as:

```
val t=Thread {System.out.println("Hello New Thread")}
t.start()
```

A small change but one that makes the code easier to read. When the lambda is passed to Thread it is automatically wrapped in an anonymous class which implements Runnable. This also means that the type that Java sees for the lambda depends on what method it is passed to.

If there is more than one possibility, or you simply want to make it clear which SAM the lambda is converted into, you can explicitly use an adapter function. These are usually generated by the compiler.

For example you can convert a lambda to a Runnable you would use:

```
val run:Runnable =  Runnable{System.out.println("Hello New Thread")}
val t=Thread (run)
t.start()
```

If you are using IntelliJ then the autocomplete will list the Java methods that accept SAMs and show you them converted into the lambda form ready for you to make use of.

Note that this automatic conversion only works for SAMs defined using an Interface and not a virtual class. Fortunately most of the important SAMs are defined as interfaces so that the classes that use them can implement more than one.

Swing Events

Now that we know how lambda's are converted to SAMs we can rewrite our Swing example so that works properly.

The system provides the invokeLater method which accepts a Runnable and runs it on the Event Dispatch Thread, EDT. Of course, we can use the same technique introduced in the previous section to avoid having to explicitly create a runnable instance:

```
SwingUtilities.invokeLater {
      val myFrame=JFrame("Hello World")
      myFrame.setSize(300,200)
      myFrame.isVisible=true
   }
```

This looks as if the SwingUtilities.invokeLater method is simply something you write your Swing code in, and in Kotlin that is how you can treat it. When the invokeLater call comes to an end, the code in our lambda is in the event queue waiting to be executed. At this point the main thread comes to an end, but our program doesn't come to an end because the event handling thread is still running, processing events and the code that you have just given it.

The only problem with this code is that when the user closes the JFrame, the EDT keeps running waiting for something to happen. We can change this behavior using the setDefaultCloseOperation method which Kotlin can use as a property:

```
SwingUtilities.invokeLater {
        val myFrame=JFrame("Hello World")
        myFrame.setSize(300,200)
        myFrame.defaultCloseOperation=JFrame.EXIT_ON_CLOSE
        myFrame.isVisible=true
    }
```

Now when you run the program it does exit when the JFrame is closed. Notice also that we have used a static property JFrame.EXIT_ON_CLOSE. This just looks like a Kotlin companion object or a Java static property depending on how you choose to look at it.

As well as displaying an empty JFrame we can also add other components such as textboxes, buttons and so on. To demonstrate how all this works, and in particular how events are handled, let's add a JButton object.

The first thing to say is that a JFrame positions components that it displays using a layout manager and the default layout manager is a border layout. This allows you to position components in fixed locations such at top left and center. If you don't want a layout manager to do the job, you can position components absolutely by giving an x,y position. This is the easiest way to start, so first we remove the default layout manager:

```
myFrame.layout=null
```

Again, this is a property converted by Kotlin from a pair of getter/setter methods.

Now we can create the JButton:

```
val myButton=JButton("Click Me")
```

and position and size it by setting its bounds rectangle by specifying the x,y pixel coordinates of the top left corner and its width and height:

```
myButton.bounds= Rectangle(15,50,150,50)
```

This is another property converted from a set/get pair, but notice that in this case the property is set to another object – a Rectangle.

Finally we can add the JButton and display the result:

```
myFrame.add(myButton)
myFrame.isVisible=true
```

The complete program is:

```
SwingUtilities.invokeLater {
      val myFrame=JFrame("Hello World")
      myFrame.setSize(300,200)
      myFrame.defaultCloseOperation=JFrame.EXIT_ON_CLOSE
      myFrame.layout=null
      val myButton=JButton("Click Me")
      myButton.bounds= Rectangle(15,50,150,50)
      myFrame.add(myButton)
      myFrame.isVisible=true
  }
```

Now we have a button, but nothing happens when you click it. To make it respond to a click we have to define an ActionListener and add it to the JButton:

```
myButton.addActionListener {
              myButton.text="You did!"
      }
```

Notice that the use of myButton within the event handler is only possible because of the closure formed when the lambda is defined and exists after the function setting up the GUI is complete.

Now when you run the program and click on the JButton, the lambda changes its text:

You can also make use of the ActionEvent object passed to the event handler to find out about the event. For example:

```
myButton.addActionListener  { e->
        myButton.text= e.source.toString()
    }
```

This prints the full Java name of the component that triggered the event.

The complete program is:

```
SwingUtilities.invokeLater {
    val myFrame=JFrame("Hello World")
    myFrame.setSize(300,200)
    myFrame.defaultCloseOperation=JFrame.EXIT_ON_CLOSE
    myFrame.layout=null
    val myButton=JButton("Click Me")
    myButton.bounds= Rectangle(15,50,150,50)
    myButton.addActionListener  { e->
            myButton.text= e.source.toString()
        }
    myFrame.add(myButton)
    myFrame.isVisible=true
}
```

This is about as far as we can go with Swing. There is a lot more to learn, but it is essentially more of the same. You can find out about layouts and other components and build up your GUI bit by bit. A good way to create a Swing GUI in Kotlin is to use NetBeans to create a layout using its interactive drag-and-drop editor, and then copy and paste the Java into your project. If you are using IntelliJ it will offer to convert the Java to Kotlin and this works reasonably well.

IDE Help

If you are using Kotlin via the IntelliJ or Android Studio IDEs you get lots of help in working out how to use Java code. Make sure that you look carefully at the autocomplete options which usually show you details of each method. You will see that properties that are generated from getters and setters are listed as being derived from particular `get` and `set` functions. You will also generally be given a list of parameters and their types. If you read all the information carefully it is usually enough to work out how to use the facility.

It is worth knowing that you can enter a reserved Kotlin keyword that can be used in Java as an ordinary identifier using backtick escapes.

For example:

```
`object`
```

is a valid Java identifier.

If you are using Android Studio then, in addition to the autocomplete and other information, there are also a number of extension methods that make life easier. If you want to know more see ***Android Programming In Kotlin: Starting with an App***.

Both Android Studio and IntelliJ have the ability to automatically convert existing Java files into Kotlin. All you have to do is open the file in a Kotlin project and select `Code, Convert To Kotlin`.

You can also convert Java snippets by pasting them into a file and accepting the offer to convert to Kotlin. The conversions are surprisingly good, but some tweaking is usually necessary. If you want to use a Java class then pasting in and converting some existing code is a good way to get a quick lesson in how to do it.

As Java types may not exist exactly in Kotlin, the IDE shows them as `T!` meaning that they could be referenced by a non-null or nullable variable, i.e. a `T` or a `T?` - see the next section. Similarly, Java collections can be treated as mutable or immutable and can be nullable or non-nullable. The IDE shows these as `(Mutable) Collection <T>!`.

Finally a Java array is shown as `Array<(out) T>!` meaning that it could be an array of a sub-type of `T` nullable or non-nullable.

Problems With Types

The biggest problem with using Java from Kotlin is that all Java types are nullable. If you assign a Java type to a Kotlin non-nullable there are no compile-time checks. The assignment might fail at run time because of a null-pointer exception or, if the assignment is to a non-null type because Kotlin added an assertion, that the assignment should be non-null.

If you rely on type inference the variable will be assigned the Java type, even though you cannot use that type in Kotlin. You can override the type inference, however, with a compatible Kotlin nullable or non-nullable type. For example, if a Java method returns a string then it is possible that the reference will be null.

You can deal with this in one of two ways.

If you set the type to a Kotlin non-nullable String using:

```
val kString:String=jString
```

then this is fine, but it could generate a run-time error as the compiler adds an assertion that jString is non-null.

If you on the other hand use a nullable Kotlin string:

```
val kString:String?=jString
```

then this will never generate a run-time error, but kString could be null and you need to check for this before you use kString.

For example, in Swing a JFrame has a property, warningString which is null unless you set it to something. If you try:

```
val myFrame=JFrame("Hello World")
var myString=myFrame.warningString
val L=myString.length
```

then the result is a NullPointerException when you run the program.

If you use:

```
val myFrame=JFrame("Hello World")
var myString:String=myFrame.warningString
val L=myString.length
```

then the result is a run-time IllegalStateException, i.e. the Kotlin compiler has added an assertion.

If you use:

```
val myFrame=JFrame("Hello World")
var myString:String?=myFrame.warningString
val L=myString.length
```

then you will see a compile-time error message saying that you have to check for null.

```
16          SwingUtilities.invokeLater {
17              val myFrame=JFrame("Hello World")
18              var myString:String?=myFrame.warningString
19              val L=myString.length
```

Only safe (?.) or non-null asserted (!!.) calls are allowed on a nullable receiver of type String?

You can make this work by checking for null in a number of possible ways. For example use:

```
val L=myString?.length
```

But after this L could be null.

It seems to be better to use a nullable type and perform the checks that are necessary than risk a run-time exception of either sort.

There is a particular, but minor, problem in working with Java arrays. Java arrays are treated as native Java arrays in Kotlin and by default they are mutable and invariant. If you need to create Java style arrays then you can use `IntArray`, `DoubleArray`, `CharArray` and so on for all primitive data types. These create basic memory mapped arrays for use in Java. Notice, however, that Kotlin compiles its own array types down to Java arrays so the difference is mostly at compile time.

The same sort of "cover up" operation is applied to primitive data types. All Java primitive data types like `int` are treated by the compiler as `Int?`. Of course, once compiled they are identical in representation anyway.

Some non-primitive types are also identical at run time and Kotlin uses the same technique of treating the Java type and the Kotlin nullable type as the same at compile time. For example, a Java enum is a Kotlin Enum!. (Recall that Kotlin shows Java types that don't have exact equivalents with a trailing exclamation mark.)

The Kotlin Principle

As you use Kotlin to consume existing Java code, the differences will seem ever more slight. Of course, mostly they are. Under the hood Kotlin tends to produce the same code that Java would – they both target the JVM and so they more or less have to.

What Kotlin does is to generate more underlying code from what you write. For example, it adds assertions that something isn't null and so on. You could have added these in Java, but you would have had to write more code.

In the same way, Kotlin converts lambdas to the appropriate anonymous class complete with a method that does the same job as the lambda. You could have written the anonymous class yourself, even using Kotlin, but it is easier to let the compiler do the work for you.

In other words, the Kotlin principle is to make use of good compile-time syntax to generate the same run-time behavior.

This was stated at the start of the book in a slightly different form, but by now it should make more sense to you.

You could say that this makes the difference between Kotlin and Java just skin deep. This is true, but don't think this is a small difference. It isn't, because it can save you a lot of time and bugs.

As long as you understand some of the principles that are behind the implementation of all languages, using Kotlin together with Java shouldn't pose any problems. This is a good reason to learn some of the fundamentals of language design and implementation.

Summary

- Working with Java from Kotlin is usually essential due to the number of existing Java libraries that applications need to use. Working with Kotlin from Java is just as easy, but not as common.

- Kotlin is a JVM language and it produces code which is very similar, if not identical, to Java. Using Java code from Kotlin is usually a matter of working out how its syntax maps to Java.

- Java's get and set methods are automatically converted to Kotlin properties. You can use the get/set methods or Kotlin's syntax to work with them.

- Kotlin can also convert Boolean functions that are named starting with is and have a setter starting with set as properties.

- Swing is still a useful Java GUI library, but like most GUI libraries it runs its UI on a separate thread from the main program – the EDT.

- Running code on the EDT is easy with the help of the SwingUtilities library.

- An Interface with a Single Abstract Method, SAM, is how Java generally implements types of functions such as event handlers. The compiler automatically converts functions passed as SAM parameters to the appropriate interface implementation. This means you can pass lambdas where a SAM is required.

- The SAM conversion means you can use lambdas as event handlers.

- The IntelliJ and Android Studio IDEs provide lots of help in working with Java including lists of methods and properties that have been automatically converted.

- Both IntelliJ and Android Studio can convert Java code files to Kotlin. You can also paste Java code into a Kotlin file with an optional conversion to Kotlin.

- Java types that don't have exact equivalents in Kotlin are shown in the IDEs as a type followed by ! .

- A particular problem with working with Java is its lack of non-nullable types. When working with a Java nullable, the best option is to treat it as a nullable Kotlin type.

- Arrays in Java are primitive data types and Kotlin provides equivalents.

- The Kotlin principle is to make use of good compile-time syntax to generate the same run-time behavior

Index

202

www.ingramcontent.com/pod-product-compliance
Lightning Source LLC
LaVergne TN
LVHW062316060326
832902LV00013B/2249